HOW TO WRITE
A
CHILDREN'S BOOK
AND
GET IT
PUBLISHED

HOW TO WRITE
A
CHILDREN'S BOOK
AND
GET IT
PUBLISHED

BARBARA SEULING

CHARLES SCRIBNER'S SONS
New York

Copyright © 1984 Barbara Seuling

Library of Congress Cataloging in Publication Data
Seuling, Barbara.
How to write a children's book and get it published.
Includes index.
Bibliography: p.
1. Children's literature — Technique. 2. Authorship.
I. Title.
PN147.5.S46   1984   808'.02   83-27124
ISBN 0-684-18055-3
0-684-18709-4 (pbk)

1 3 5 7 9 11 13 15 17 19   F/P   20 18 16 14 12 10 8 6 4 2

Printed in the United States of America.

The quotation on page 5, by Madeleine L'Engle, is from a paper given at the annual conference of the Louisiana Library Association in 1964.

Portions of Chapter 14, "For the Writer Who Is Also an Illustrator," have appeared previously in a publication of the Society of Children's Book Writers.

Cover illustration of Rat by Ernest H. Shepard from *The Wind in the Willows.*

for

SUE ALEXANDER

my special friend

You write not for children but for yourself. And if by good fortune children enjoy what you enjoy, why then you are a writer of children's books . . . no special credit to you, but simply thumping good luck!
—*Arthur Ransome*

Contents

Acknowledgments

My thanks to some good friends who supported and endured, with patience and humor, throughout the writing of this book: Winnette Glasgow, Sue Alexander, Phil Seuling, Gwenn Seuling, Beth Teitelman, and Isaiah Bard.

Introduction

Do YOU WANT to write a children's book? Are you excited by the idea of writing for children and the possibility of being published, but not sure how to begin or where to send your material?

Perhaps you want to immortalize a long-loved story, made up to amuse the children, or to remember and preserve tales told to you by *your* elders, complete with details of lives and places that exist no more. Possibly you live or work with children on a daily basis—as a parent, or teacher, or librarian—and after seeing and reading a great number of books want to try your hand at writing one of your own.

Whatever the reasons, writing for children has undeniable appeal and its own satisfactions—but how *do* you begin? What do you do to break through that mysterious barrier that seems to exist between writer and publisher?

In the five sections ahead, you will learn what to do with your ideas and ambition. First, you are guided to the world of children's books and publishing as preparation for your job as a writer; second, you are shown how to develop your ideas, do the research, and propose ideas to publishers professionally; third, you set out to explore writing techniques that work and ways to judge your work critically; fourth, you learn about the market and how to act as your own agent in locating the right publisher; finally, you learn what to expect from agents, contracts, your editor and publisher, and how to become a part of the community of writers.

These insights and observations from my own experience may help you avoid some of the difficulties met by most beginners. Perhaps I can help you to plot a novel, or to see how characters can be turned from cardboard into flesh and blood, but the biggest lessons will be learned as you put your words on paper day after day and have them come out with the elusive quality that makes the reader think, see, and feel.

There are hundreds of children's periodicals and about 150 children's book publishers continuously in need of new material. If you have talent for writing and communicating with young readers and are willing to study, work hard, and learn, you can work your way toward publication, where you will be among the most sincere and genuinely contented writers I know—those who write for young people.

HOW TO WRITE
A
CHILDREN'S BOOK
AND
GET IT
PUBLISHED

Part One

A CLOSER LOOK AT CHILDREN'S BOOKS

A good book respects a child's intelligence, his pride, his dignity, and most of all his individuality and his capacity to become....
—*Jean Karl,* From Childhood to Childhood

1

You, the Children's Book Writer . . . Maybe

CAN YOU DEFINE your goals as a children's writer? What do you want to achieve? Be honest. Do you want to make a lot of money? Tell wonderful stories? Become a better writer? Organize your ideas? Quit your job and write children's books for a living? Become famous? Weave fantasies? Explore how things work? Communicate with a younger generation?

Writers write for various reasons, some because they must, others to feel a sense of permanence, still others to explore their own abilities in communicating, and some just because writing is fun. Writers are often compelled by many reasons but, when cornered, admit to one or two, such as the above.

First, figure out what your goals are. Then, look at yourself squarely to see how near or far you are from those goals.

Are you ready and willing to work hard? Are you willing to be taught? (Being eager to learn is not the same thing.) Is your desire to write for children strong enough to withstand difficult times? Are you strongly motivated to succeed so you will stick with writing when it gets tougher? Are you flexible in your attitudes, open to suggestion and criticism?

Do you have talent? Don't be modest about this. We usually know by the time we reach adolescence whether or not we are talented; significant observers such as parents, teachers, and friends tell us, and we can usually measure ourselves to some degree against our peers.

Can you work alone? If you have never worked in isolation, you may be surprised. With no one around for input or feedback, no voices, no bodies moving around, you can feel pretty lonely. When I first began freelancing after many years in an office, I nearly went out of my mind with the lack of human sounds and movement. I finally hung a full-length mirror at the other end of the room where my reflection seemed like another person working. It was five years before I told anyone about it, I felt so weird.

Do you have what it takes to write for children? Please don't say that you want to write for children because it is easier than, or you are not skilled enough yet for, writing adult books. Say that to a children's book writer and you will cause varying degrees of anxiety, manifested by anything from a gritting of teeth to the tearing out of hair.

Children's books are *not* watered-down adult books. They demand certain abilities of their authors, not the least of which is that of being able to tap into the minds and souls of young people without intruding, and to project the voice of those young people to the reader. You, as an experienced adult, have to see things objectively and yet have the ability to recall feelings and attitudes and viewpoints of your early years to the point that you can write about them convincingly. Charlotte Zolotow, retired editorial director of Harper and Row's Young Readers Department and well-known author, calls it "a kind of double-exposure"—being aware of something as an adult and remembering what it was like as a child.

4

Not all of us can write for children; some cultivate the ability with effort. We must constantly step back and wriggle into the shoes and the skin of the child before writing, yet we must craft our language with grown-up care, not to deplete it of its excitement and color, giving the young reader much to absorb and digest. Most successful children's book writers are skilled naturally, but some only for a particular age group to which they seem to have a direct line. A rare few can write for several age groups and in various categories. We are a mixed breed, but we *choose* to write for children; we do not resign ourselves to a subordinate publishing group. I like Madeleine L'Engle's reply, when asked why she wrote books for children: "You have to write whatever book it is that wants to be written. And then, if it's going to be too difficult for grown-ups, you write it for children."

What have you read? When was the last time you read a children's book? You cannot be ready to write for children if you don't even know what kind of books are being written these days. Who are the authors most popular with children? Whose writing style do you like best? If you could spend a week with three children's book writers to learn all the tricks of the trade, which ones would you choose?

Start by reading all the books you can handle. If you need help in choosing books, there are some very good book lists available. Several are listed in Appendix I.

Read old books and new ones, popular stories and literary classics, good ones and bad. Choose a variety of titles from novels, picture books, non-fiction, how-to books, photo essays, joke and riddle books. If the person next to you on the bus is reading the latest steamy adult best seller while you are laughing over Richard and Florence Atwater's *Mr. Popper's Penguins,* don't worry; you will get used to it in time. Soon you will be so absorbed in what you are reading that you will hardly notice anyone else on the bus and you may even miss your stop. Besides, isn't it reassuring that *Mr. Popper's Penguins* is still in print and as popular as ever after more than forty years, while most popular adult novels are forgotten in a year?

Sometimes you will like a book personally but feel that it is not right for children. Why? Whose work represents most closely the work that you would like to do? Are you drawn to the books of one publisher over and over again? After a while you will notice a pattern and learn that you can identify by their type and looks the books of the publisher with whom you feel an affinity. When you consider that there are about 150 publishers, your attraction to one or three or even six is significant. You clearly recognize something in those publishing houses that is especially right for you, a kinship that will probably urge you, one day, to submit your own manuscripts to them before any others.

Dig deeper and deeper as you read, and pose difficult questions for yourself. Are wordless picture books as effective as those with a text? Do you see any disadvantages? When does a picture book seem too long? What makes a book remain popular over the years?

How do styles differ? How does Beverly Cleary hold the attention of the 8-year-old who grew up on a steady diet of TV? Why are Judy Blume's books so popular with pre-teens? How is her style different from Joan Aiken's or Katherine Paterson's or Betsy Byars's? How do the Cleavers, Vera and Bill, draw characters, young people, struggling with fierce burdens? How does M. E. Kerr make you laugh all the way through a book and still say something important and serious? How do different authors handle anger in a child? Loneliness? Abandonment? Fear? Joy?

Exercises like these will help to sharpen your critical sense, which will later enable you to judge your own work more effectively. At the same time, you will become much more aware of children's books and publishing in general.

6

Incidentally, don't avoid reading books that you don't like. In the past you have probably just put down books that did not interest you. Now, examine *why* you would like to put a book down. You can learn a great deal from this critical look. Perhaps you will uncover a weakness in your own work as you uncover it in someone else's writing and will be able to avoid that weakness in the future.

Do you know how to type? I cannot conceive of any serious writer not knowing how to type, but I'm sure there are some. It is to your advantage to learn this skill, since publishers will not read handwritten manuscripts.

Soon, it appears, typewriters will give way to word processors, and if you are just starting out, you may find it easier to learn word processing than typing. With a word processor you will "write" your book on a computer, and the machine's memory will store what you type so that you can call it back at any time, make changes, add sections, and so on. By punching in different commands, you can make corrections, switch paragraphs around, change characters' names throughout the work, and even page and index the work. All of this simplifies the keyboard gymnastics for you, but you can't get away from having to learn at least the rudiments of the keyboard, which is the same for a typewriter as for a word processor. Writers who use word processors find that they take time to learn and use but save weeks of typing and revision time on each book.

What have you already accomplished toward becoming a children's book writer? Consider your school background and your outside interests. What was your favorite subject? English? Psychology? History? What are your hobbies and interests? Playing the guitar? Magic? Stamp collecting? Any and all of these help you as a children's book writer. What jobs have you had? Fireman? Animal trainer? Baby-sitter? Pilot? Speech therapist? Skating instructor? Popcorn vendor? Any job gives you a closer look at some special area, its people and its atmosphere and its peculiarities. Some may be especially help-ful because of their relation to children or books, but others give you insights into human behavior.

All life experiences are your training ground for writing. Anything you see and absorb now may one day be recalled for a location, a character, a development in a relationship, a motivation, or a supportive detail. Your perceptions and judg-ments will have a direct bearing on what you choose to write about, and how you say what you feel.

Do you have the patience to learn, the stomach for criticism, and the tolerance for difficult times? Are you willing to wait until you are ready to be published, to learn the skills you need and to put in the time gaining insight and experience? And then, do you have the stamina to persist, undaunted, through possible rejections, before your work is accepted? These, per-haps, are the most crucial issues to confront, for if you come up positive in every other way but have not allowed for the patience and foresight to train yourself or to be trained well, you will lose heart at your first rejection and go down defeated before you have had a chance. It happens to many people because they are not realistic about the necessary hard work that it takes for the success they are seeking.

SUGGESTIONS—CHAPTER 1

1. Start reading! Choose one or more book lists from Appen-dix I and send for them. Look up the works of the authors mentioned in this chapter while you wait for them to arrive:

Joan Aiken	Judy Blume
Richard and Florence Atwater	Betsy Byars
	Beverly Cleary

8

Vera and Bill Cleaver   Katherine Paterson

M. E. Kerr   Charlotte Zolotow

Madeleine L'Engle

Read critically. Is it a good story? Are the characters inter-esting? Is the ending satisfying? Is the plot clear? If it is a picture book, how do the illustrations play their part in the overall view of the book?

2. List some life experiences you have had that could serve as background material for a story.

2

What Is a Children's Book?

WHEN YOU SAY "children's book," what pops into your mind? Do you have an image of a big, colorful picture book that you can read to a child sitting on your lap? Do you think of a fat mystery story—perhaps a Nancy Drew or a Hardy Boys story—that is perfect for a rainy summer afternoon? Or do you think of a how-to or a what's-that kind of book that shows you how to build your own science lab or skyscraper or what makes a shark grow two sets of teeth or where you can find buried treasure? Are children's books, to you, bits of fluff, cute little pastimes wrapped in a pretty package?

Chances are, no matter what your personal image of a children's book is, you are not thinking of any of the following:

1. a graphically explicit book about the atomic bomb attack on Hiroshima for picture-book age
2. a guide to young people's legal rights in regard to drinking, driving, voting, and marriage

3. a novel about a young girl who is raped by a disturbed teenager who wants to "teach her a lesson"
4. an adventure story set in the Himalayas in which the reader is the hero and can choose his own ending

All of these are children's books and can be considered representative of the current children's market. They may not meet your image of what a children's book is, and not everyone will choose them for personal reading pleasure, but the fact that they are available tells you something about where we are in the publishing of children's books today. It also tells you that the image of "the cute little book" for children is not accurate. As we read stories that stretch our imaginations and tell us of other times and places, we also read about the family of mankind and the social issues that beset our age. There are also books that can be zipped, laundered, scratched, and smelled, without harm to the book, and some that open up into three-dimensional toys. The point is, there are many kinds of books for children, with a depth and scope never before imagined, so it is truly impossible to fix on only one kind when you discuss children's books.

Although you may have one kind of book in mind that you want to write, you are entering a field that is small enough to know intimately, but that is vast and diverse in its range. It is important that you know at least what the different types of books are for reference in reading and communicating, later, with editors and other writers. Following is a brief rundown of the kinds of books published today.

PICTURE BOOKS

For the youngest children, up to about age 6 or 7, these include word and counting books and concept books for the younger years, as well as nursery rhymes, picture identification books, and wordless books. Books are usually read aloud to the youngest children by adults. Once a book has been read to a child, he will go back to it many times on his own, using pictures to provide clues to the text. Older children in this age range read picture books on their own, usually those with good solid stories. Pictures are crucial for this age. Examples: *Goodnight Moon* by Margaret Wise Brown, illustrated by Clement Hurd; *ABC* by John Burningham; *The Best Word Book Ever* by Richard Scarry (for younger children); *Bedtime for Frances* by Russell Hoban, illustrated by Garth Williams; *One Monday Morning* by Uri Shulevitz; *Amos and Boris* by William Steig (for older children).

EASY READERS

A popular genre, it was created especially for the first- and second-grade child just learning to read and the third grader who is not yet comfortable with longer, more difficult reading material. They are available in a variety of categories—history, science, mysteries, stories—and enable the youngest reader to read on his own. Great care is taken to give these books an older look, distinct from picture books. Examples: *Little Bear* by Else Holmelund Minarik, illustrated by Maurice Sendak; *Witch, Goblin, and Sometimes Ghost* by Sue Alexander, illustrated by Tomie de Paola; *The Cat in the Hat* by Dr. Seuss; *Pippa Mouse* by Bette Boegehold, illustrated by Cyndy Szekeres; *Octopus* by Evelyn S. Shaw, illustrated by Ralph Carpentier; *Wagon Wheels* by Barbara Brenner, illustrated by Don Bolognese.

"MIDDLE-AGE" FICTION

So called because it is for readers in the middle grades, 3 to 6, or ages 8 to 11, this wide span accommodates the hungriest reading ages, with interests ranging from adventure and fantasy to family stories and historical settings. This group needs action and a solid story with an uncomplicated plot. Costs prohibit pictures in recent books; this is sad, since readers in this age group like occasional illustrations. Examples: *Encyclopedia Brown, Boy Detective* by Donald J. Sobol; *Where the Lilies Bloom* by Vera and Bill Cleaver; *Henry Huggins* by Beverly Cleary; *My Side of the Mountain* by Jean Craighead George; *Charlotte's Web* by E. B. White.

"MIDDLE-AGE" NON-FICTION

This is for an age whose appetite for straightforward information on any and all subjects is enormous. Readers are brutally alert to errors and omissions. Pictorial material is essential to clarify subject matter. The text must be lively and well-organized and concepts should be within the understanding and experience of the reader. Examples: *Shark Lady* by Ann McGovern; *Animal Fact/Animal Fable* by Seymour Simon; *A Snake-Lover's Diary* by Barbara Brenner; *Chimney Sweeps* by James C. Giblin; *Eclipse: Darkness in Daytime* by Franklyn M. Branley; *Drawing and Painting with the Computer* by Don Bolognese.

TEENAGE OR "YOUNG ADULT" FICTION

More advanced in style and plot than younger fiction, with more attention to detail, the stories deal with more complicated relationships, values, and feelings. Some romance might be involved, but sex, while acknowledged, is not usually explicit. Heroes and heroines are young people of junior high or high school age. No subject matter is taboo; good taste is all-important. Examples: *Tiger Eyes* by Judy Blume; *Annie on My Mind* by Nancy Garden; *Little Little* by M. E. Kerr; *Jacob Have I Loved* by Katherine Paterson; *Homecoming* by Cynthia Voigt; *Edith Jackson* by Rosa Guy.

TEENAGE NON-FICTION

Written in a lively and readable style, the subject matter is chosen to appeal to readers old enough to be stimulated into probing and understanding major ideas. The information relates to the experience of young people and assumes little or no previous knowledge of the subject. Examples: *To Be a Slave* by Julius Lester; *Bionic Parts for People* by Gloria Skurzynski; *Black Magic, White Magic* by Gary Jennings; *Loss and How to Cope with It* by Joanne Bernstein; *The Genetics Explosion* by Dr. Alvin and Virginia B. Silverstein; *Finding Your First Job* by Sue Alexander.

HI-LO BOOKS

This is a fairly recent creation by publishers to meet the needs of the reader who is reading below grade level but who wants interesting reading material. The "hi-lo" stands for "high interest/low reading level." It includes fiction and non-fiction and is often illustrated with photos to ease the reader along. Stories are ususlly contemporary, packed with fast action, humor, and romance; dialogue is short and quick, and issues are uncomplicated within a strong plot line. Examples:

Hit and Run by Linda Atkinson; *Mystery of the Mummy's Mask* by Florence Parry Heide and Sylvia Van Clief; *Invasion: 2200 A.D.* by Howard Goldsmith; *Danger! White Water* by Otto Penzier; *Super-Champions of Ice Hockey* by Ross R. Olney; *Dracula, Go Home* by Kin Platt.

NOVELTY

This refers to books that fit no other category, such as puzzle and game books, miniature books in boxed sets, pop-ups, activity and shape books, books that open up into toys, books that can be patted, smelled, and thrown in the bathtub. Some of these are published by book publishers, others are manufactured by toy companies. All go under the name of "book" if they can be read in the traditional way. Examples: *Dragons* by David Kawami (a punch-out book of models); *The Nutshell Library* by Maurice Sendak (three miniature books in a boxed set); *Mix and Match* books (pages that separate into sections so you can mix them up); *Robot* by Jan Pienkowsky (a pop-up book); the *Choose Your Own Adventure* series by Bantam Books (you choose the ending); *Animal Crackers* by Carolyn Bracken (riddles and jokes).

You will surely think of still other categories, such as plays, anthologies, and poetry. Poetry is always popular with children, and some delightful collections abound by authors with strong reputations, but this is hard ground to break for a beginner. For our purposes, the above list should prove sufficient.

If your view of children's books is slightly shaken, don't be alarmed: it has simply expanded, rather quickly. Most people who are not intimately involved with books every day are surprised at the broad range of books now available to young people. Publishers still emphasize care and taste in selecting manuscripts that will provide a wide range of fiction and non-fiction for the young reader.

Most editors, I am happy to say, still try to satisfy the sense of wonder and delight in the youngest readers, the curiosity in older ones, and to maintain the trust of all readers by providing accurate information by way of the finest writing available.

SUGGESTIONS—CHAPTER 2

1. Look up several subjects in the *Subject Guide to Books in Print* and the *Subject Guide to Children's Books in Print*—friendship, dinosaurs, computers, China, modern art—to get an idea of the range of books available on a single subject.

2. Get a small notebook that you can tuck in a pocket or purse and carry with you at all times. Keep the front of the book for notes on your readings, recording author, illustrator, publisher, and year of publication for each book you read, plus something significant, positive or negative, about the book. Allow only two lines for each book for all of this; the briefer it is, the more you will remember it. In the back of the notebook, jot down observations from life or flashes of good ideas for stories or physical characteristics or any quirks of behavior you may see that can be used in your writings later. Use this notebook often, the way an artist uses a sketchbook. Aim to fill it up quickly and move on to another one.

3

How to Become an Expert

It is a sad fact that to get a work published, talent is not always enough. Many talented writers drop out of sight when the going gets rough. Often, they do not understand the publishing system, cannot bear the rejection letters, and are frustrated by the long wait for a decision. Those who meet the challenges with intelligence and determination are generally the ones who succeed.

Perhaps you have heard about someone whose first manuscript was accepted on its first submission to a publisher. Such things do happen, rarely, and you do not hear the part about how much time the author spent researching, writing the book, and rewriting again and again. Often there are years of work leading up to the "overnight success."

Of course talent plays a part; it always does, but if your ego is thin and bruises easily, or if you cannot accept rejection, this is not the field for you. Many professional writers know for a fact that they will average six to ten rejections before a publisher takes on a project. Madeleine L'Engle sent *A Wrinkle in Time* around fourteen times before it was accepted and went on to win the Newbery Medal, the highest award for achievement in children's writing. Twenty-eight publishers rejected Dr. Seuss's *And to Think I Saw It on Mulberry Street* before it found its publisher and fame for its author. Some careers would never have begun had the creators been overly sensitive and given up after early rejection.

Rejection letters are part of the game. They are not sent to hurt but to inform you. A return of your manuscript means, simply, that your work is not right for that particular publisher at that particular time, just as the letter says. If you are unreasonably disappointed, you have not prepared yourself properly. What you need to know is what experienced and skilled writers have learned over the years—that publishing is a business and that editors must react to material with that business always in mind. What suits one editor on a personal level may not suit the sales director, who knows that he will not be able to sell the book, or the editor in chief, who feels the book does not fit the publisher's image. In the end, an acquisition is a team decision, even when only one person holds the ultimate responsibility. The editor must take into account what the rest of the company feels it can do for the book in the way of production, promotion, and sales.

Learning something about the *business* of children's books, then, should be part of your training as a children's book writer. It can be as important to you as writing well, and will be one of your most valuable tools in the long run.

BROWSE THE BOOKSHELVES

The public library is an excellent resource, but you may not find the latest books. It can take months to order, catalog, and shelve the newest books. Depending on the library's budget, the book you want may not have been purchased at all. What you *can* find in the library, however, are the well-worn best-loved books of previous years, and a great deal of non-fiction that never makes it to the bookstores. You also have the advantage of the children's librarian, who knows the needs of a whole community of young readers and has a picture of the reading tastes of children discovering and choosing their own books.

If it isn't too busy a day, ask the librarian some questions. What do the gifted readers like to read? Are there books for bilingual children? Do award-winning books move off the shelves faster than other books? When a child asks for a "funny" book, what is recommended? When there are budget concerns, which books are the first to be eliminated from purchasing consideration? How does a librarian select the books from among the thousands that are published each year? How many of them are actually read before purchase?

While you are spending this pleasant and informative time at the library, you will be learning a great deal about the biggest market for children's book publishing: the library.

For the most recent books, the bookstore is the place to go. When choosing a bookstore, however, be sure to find one that has a well-stocked, representative children's book department. The standard shopping mall stores do not, nor do many others that cater mostly to adults. Sometimes they will keep a few "classics" or best sellers around to satisfy customers who want to pick up something for a child while doing their own book buying. In these cases, there are generally a few battle-worn classics such as *Black Beauty* and *Heidi*, and some mass-produced ABC or dictionary-style picture-and-word books that are cheaply produced and run off on giant presses to keep the costs down. There is nothing wrong with these books, but they do not represent children's books any more than Coney Island represents New York City. Some bookstore owners, alas, are so sure that people won't spend "real" money on books for children that the sparsity of good books is perpetuated. Others, thank heaven, have proven them wrong, but old habits are hard to change. Publishers are now finding that this market is worth some additional thought and are making an effort to educate the public about the value of buying books of quality for children. After all, a picture book that costs $12.95 lasts a lot longer than most plastic toys that you can buy for the same amount of money, and the book has far greater value in the long run.

Also beware of discount bookstores that feature a children's book department. They may buy overstock or remainders, and so their selection is not at all typical. Your town may have an exceptionally good independent bookstore with a full, rich, up-to-date children's department. Such shops are treasures and usually have staffs to match. Dedicated owners invite book people to visit for book-signing events, storytelling, and talks. Eeyore's in New York City is one such place: another is the Northshire Book Shop in Manchester, Vermont. Such places are worth searching for.

By now you are probably aware of a major factor in the book business: children's books are mostly bought by adults—parents, librarians, teachers, family friends—who control the money and make the purchasing decisions, even though the ultimate judge of the book is still the child. This makes selling a children's book a double-barreled challenge: not only do you have to satisfy the child reader but the grown-up reader and buyer as well.

STUDY THE PUBLISHERS

The next thing to do is to take a closer look at the publishers. Learn who they are and what their books are like. You can find a listing of them in a directory casually known as the "LMP," short for *Literary Market Place.* Your library should have a copy of it. You will also find a listing in *The Writer's Handbook* or *Writer's Market.* The Children's Book Council has its own member listing available on request (see Appendix IV).

Publishers print catalogs of their new books, which generally come out in two seasons, spring and fall. These are mailed to public and school libraries across the country, as well as to bookstores, children's literature specialists, and the media. Some librarians decide on their purchases through the information supplied in these catalogs. Salesmen who visit libraries and stores use the catalog as an introduction, then visit with samples (book jackets, proofs, and so on) of the actual books. You can get quite a good picture of each book from the information in the catalog—size, shape, color, and special qualities, along with a brief summary of the book's content and something about the author and illustrator. Write to publishers requesting their latest catalogs and ask to be put on their mailing lists. Also, your children's librarian may have a collection of catalogs on hand that you can look at.

You can learn a great deal by studying catalogs. You can judge the character of a publishing house by examining its books season after season. It will soon be clear to you which publisher is seeking the new and different and which is hanging on to the traditional, which specializes in fiction and which publishes only non-fiction. You will see which one introduces new authors regularly and which house is emphasizing contemporary novels, mysteries, or romances. Most publishers do a variety of books for all ages, but within that very general framework you can see preferences and priorities.

21

REVIEW THE REVIEWERS

To find new books that might interest you or to learn something about the latest trends in publishing, read reviews of current children's books. The best sources of these are a handful of trade publications that can be found in most libraries. They are: *School Library Journal*, the *Horn Book, Booklist,* and the *Bulletin of the Center for Children's Books.* Two other sources, the *New York Times Book Review* and *Publishers Weekly*, periodically devote a large part of their magazine to children's books, as well as a small part on a weekly basis. Just browsing through the special issues is informative.

A detailed list of reviewers appears in Appendix II.

THE CHILDREN'S BOOK COUNCIL

This nonprofit organization (address in Appendix VII) is devoted to supporting and promoting quality books for children. Among other things they sponsor National Children's Book Week and produce bookmarks, posters, and mobiles to promote books and reading. The council makes available to writers and illustrators information and advice on how to present work to publishers for consideration. Details on its various literature (some of it free) appear throughout this book.

The library of the council is a collection of books published by the major children's book publishers over the last three years and is open to the public for browsing. If you happen to be in the New York area, you can visit the council headquarters and see firsthand what is being published today. If you cannot make a personal visit, be sure to send for the literature described in the chapters ahead. An additional publication, CBC Features, published irregularly with news and information about children, will be sent to you indefinitely for a one-time fee of $25.00.

Browsing and reading in all the right places, you will be amazed at how much background information you can and will pick up and how good you will feel armed with this vast amount of new knowledge, changing you from a passive observer to an involved participant and, ultimately, to an expert.

SUGGESTIONS—CHAPTER 3

1. Send a letter and a stamped self-addressed envelope to the Children's Book Council, 67 Irving Place, New York, NY 10003, for a handy listing called "Members' Publishing Programs," which provides names and addresses and brief summaries of what the publishers are doing. When the listing arrives, read through it to find publishers whose catalogs you would like to see, and send away for them. You may also find publishers catalogs at your public library.

2. If you want an attractive, well-organized catalog from a serious children's bookstore, Eeyore's (2252 Broadway, New York, NY 10024) has one available that gives you the feeling of browsing through its cheerful shelves in person. Send $1 for postage and handling.

3. Seek out a copy of the *Horn Book* (your library should have it) and look through it carefully; it has articles related to children's books and a major section on reviews of the latest children's books. You can either look it up regularly or subscribe to it, but do keep in touch with it.

4

*Lessons from the Past**

THE BOOK WRITTEN just for children—for their enjoyment—is commonplace today but is a relatively new development in literature. First, we had to learn as a society to allow
ourselves the pleasure of expanding our minds and our vision
and to trust that in sharing tools of enrichment with our
children, no harm would come to them. This came with difficulty after our Puritan beginnings and through the influence
of Victorian times.

There were a few exceptions, among them John Newberry's

* For those aspiring writers who have no knowledge of the development of
children's books, I am including a brief chapter to sketch in some of the rich
beginnings and important movements that have affected the way we perceive
the children's book today. Experts and those with some background in this
field will surely find this cursory look at the history of children's books lacking
in many important features. Those who are interested can make a deeper
study by reading some of the many fine books on the subject listed in Appendix III.

A *Little Pretty Pocket Book*, an entertaining mixture of poems, pictures, and stories for little children, published in England in 1794. Before that, illustrated versions of *Aesop's Fables*, published for adults, were shared with a few fortunate children, as was Charles Perrault's collection of *Fairy Tales*, published in France in 1697.

The picture got better in the nineteenth century. There was Edward Lear's nonsense verse, Lewis Carroll's *Alice in Wonderland*, and a few picture books by Walter Crane, Kate Greenaway, and Randolph Caldecott in England. In America, Louisa May Alcott and Mark Twain wrote works for adults that were immediately snatched up by children, and Clement C. Moore wrote *A Visit from St. Nicholas* just for young people.

This period was one of prim propriety, so along with the few treasures above came many dreary publications emphasizing the three Rs, religious instruction, or the various virtues, disguised, sometimes, in heartrending melodrama. If you look at some story titles in books published during this time, you'll find ones like these: "Blind Arthur and His Sister Jane," "Be Brave When the Trial Comes," and "Brave Little Heart." Still, to the children of the time, having stories of their own, even preachy ones, must have been a thrill.

In 1873, Scribners in New York published a magazine just for children. It was packed with stories, poems, pictures, humor, puzzles, and games, and it was called *St. Nicholas Magazine*. Edited by Mary Mapes Dodge, an author with excellent taste and vision, *St. Nicholas* blossomed, drawing the finest writers of the day, among them Louisa May Alcott (*Little Women*), L. Frank Baum (the *Oz* books), Rudyard Kipling (*The Jungle Books*), Frances Hodgson Burnett (*The Secret Garden*), and Joel Chandler Harris (*Nights with Uncle Remus*). *St. Nicholas* was the true forerunner of children's publishing in America. In 1919, Macmillan opened the first children's book department; others followed shortly after.

In the 1930s, children's books belonged to the illustrators. It was the time of Ludwig Bemelmans (*Madeleine*), Wanda Gag (*Millions of Cats*), Robert Lawson (*The Story of Ferdinand* by Munro Leaf), and James Daugherty (*Andy and the Lion*).

By the 1940s, the emphasis had shifted from picture books to longer stories. From that period came these: *The Moffats* by Eleanor Estes, *Rabbit Hill* by Robert Lawson, *Homer Price* by Robert McCloskey, and *The 21 Balloons* by William Pène du Bois, to name just a few. Imaginations were wide open, and children explored colorful, magical, mysterious other worlds through books, stretching their minds and their dreams, but always with the warm reassurance that everything came out right in the end.

A visit to the library today will show just how solid those books were—and still are. Many of them are still popular, worn and dog-eared with use. Picture books produced in black and white, under the restrictions of Depression budgets, are still as attractive to children as the more elaborate full-color books produced in recent years. Many are in the fiftieth reprinting. It is a short education in itself to look at these books, read them, and understand the simple success of them—the essence of what is good in children's books.

The 1950s brought us Dr. Seuss and a shy but imaginative Danish-American schoolteacher named Else Holmelund Minarik.

Dr. Seuss had been around for years, captivating children with his wonderful silly rhymes and equally silly but charming pictures. The new wrinkle was a book that was especially created for the beginning reader, using words the reader could recognize. Up to that time the only reading materials for a beginning reader were dreary school textbooks of the Dick-and-Jane variety. Dr. Seuss's book was *The Cat in the Hat*. In nonsense verse and hilarious pictures, Seuss created a marvelous mess (and cleaned it up again, to the relief of parents), all

the while giving the brand-new reader a bit of fun and pleasure with his new skill—reading—as the textbooks rarely did.

At just about the same time that Dr. Seuss was writing *The
Cat in the Hat,* Else Holmelund Minarik was writing *Little
Bear* in answer to the desperate need of her first-grade stu-
dents to use their newly learned reading skills to "read" something satisfying, not a school text but a "real" book, on their
own. Minarik created a character, Little Bear, who behaves
much like any active 6-year-old going through his daily antics.
Minarik's book inspired enthusiasm and confidence in the
youngest readers, with stories about Little Bear and Mother,
Little Bear and his friends, and other familiar and cozy settings.

The Cat in the Hat and *Little Bear* were both published in
1957, beginning a whole new genre of books for children. Both
Seuss's and Minarik's styles were eagerly accepted by children
and widely imitated in subsequent years by just about every
publishing house with a children's department. Today, the
easy-to-read book is a standard category in many publishing
programs.

Then came the 1960s and the emergence of a genius named
Maurice Sendak . . . and after that, every picture book was
inevitably compared to the work of Sendak.

Sendak had begun his career in an apprenticeship role under the wing of Ursula Nordstrom of Harper and Row. Nordstrom discovered him while he was decorating windows for
F.A.O. Schwarz, the toy emporium on Fifth Avenue, and invit-
ed him to illustrate children's books. Some of those early works
include Ruth Kraus's *A Hole Is to Dig,* Meindert de Jong's *The
House of Sixty Fathers,* and Else Minarik's *Little Bear* books.
Eventually he wrote his own book, *Kenny's Window,* and four
tiny books in a box called *The Nutshell Library,* which has
been a best-selling item in children's book departments ever
since. Still, it was not until 1963 that everyone sat up and took

notice of this amazing talent. In that year, *Where the Wild Things Are* was published.

To look at the book is to see all that a children's book should and could be . . . the true quality of book magic. Text and pictures work so harmoniously that when, for several pages, there are no words at all, the reader is hardly aware of their absence. Low-key colors and fine draftsmanship are far more appealing than eye-dazzling colors and shapes. The basis for the book is the psychologically sound story of Max, who is punished for being noisy and wild and talking back by being sent to his room. There he imagines that he sails off to a place where the wild things are, with himself, Max, in charge of them all. When he grows tired of the wild things, he comes home again to his little room, where he finds his dinner waiting for him, still warm.

Sendak designed the double-spread pages to lure the reader into their depths without ever being aware—you see how the size of the drawing grows with each page until the exciting climax, then dwindles again until Max is back in his room. You watch the trees grow out of the bedposts and push out of the frame of the picture as Max's imagination pushes him away from the humdrum, restricted atmosphere of home to a place where all things are allowed and he is in command . . . every child's fantasy.

All of these factors are important to the book's whole and reasons for its success. There are some who say that the wild things scare little children, that some readers are afraid when they read the book. Those children should not be given the book to read. For most other children, the book is sheer delight, slightly dizzying with its implications of freedom and dangers never before experienced. The fact that everything comes right back home again where Max is safe and warm and someone cares seems to make up for the exhilarating and dangerous adventure and keeps the wild things safely in their place. (Isn't it also splendid that Sendak has them far away on a remote island and leaves them far behind when Max returns home, implying that the wild things are not near enough to harm us; and isn't it clever that the worst thing the wild things do is make a lot of noise and gnash their terrible teeth and roll their terrible eyes? There is nothing vicious about them, but children, with their wild and lively imaginations, probably see much more in their potential than we poor unseeing adults do.)

Sendak's arrival on the picture book scene may have had something to do with picture book production reaching an important technological peak. Also, the economy was healthy, and schools and public libraries all across the country were buying books in large numbers. The government fed money for additional book purchases into the systems, and print orders were high. Color reproduction became better than it had ever been to keep up with the demands of such illustrators as Sendak and Uri Shulevitz and Marcia Brown and Blair Lent. Advances were made in the quality of paper used in book production, reproduction techniques, and even in the printing inks themselves. Prices were stable, and for $3.95 you could expect a large, full-color picture book with a clothbound binding under its paper dust jacket.

A comparison of the books of the 1930s and 1940s with the books published in the mid-1960s and into the 1980s will give you a good understanding of the major changes that have taken place from one period to another. You will see, for example, our innocence as a nation before World War II through our stories and attitudes; and as we became a nation obsessed by issues, so our books became outlets for dealing with those matters. Suddenly there were books about blacks and native Americans and civil rights; about sexuality in all its aspects; about crime and poverty and urban development. These gave way in time to books about women's liberation and unpopular wars. As the mores of our society have stretched to accommodate divorce and remarriage as a viable way of life, books about children of divorce and stepparents began to emerge. Joan Lexau's story of a boy waiting for a letter from his father in *Me Day*, Judy Blume's *It's Not the End of the World*, about a family facing divorce, and Paula Danziger's *Divorce Express*, about a teenage girl who must break up her life to commute every weekend to see her dad in New York City, are all representative of this age of restructured families.

You will also see from this exploration that in the 1970s, costs of books skyrocketed. Our uncertain economy threw the prices of paper, printing, and labor way up, and publishers had to find ways to keep prices down, so there is a visible change in quality of bindings and use of color, two of the more expensive areas in book production. (It is interesting to note, that the 1982 Caldecott Medal for the most distinguished picture book went to Chris Van Allsburg for *Jumanji*, a picture storybook illustrated entirely in black and white. Children's book artists seem always to rise to the challenge of restrictions.)

There are exciting things happening in children's books again today. Computer technology has forced new thinking into every aspect of publishing, and in the next few years we should see some interesting by-products of this revolutionary change. Writers will be able to use word processors to write and modems to transmit their work to publishers without ever having to type them on paper first. Publishers will be able to send disks or tapes to printers to have books set in type. Only the binding seems, so far, to have escaped the influence of the computer, but even that may change.

Rather than run from these strange-sounding ideas, keep your mind open to them. Understanding how publishing— even electronic publishing—works and how publishers make their decisions to buy the work of writers is as important to you as the talent with which you came to writing in the first place and the skills you have developed along the way. If writing is to be your business, remaining in the dark ages about decisions that could affect publishing will cheat you out of an important part of your professional training.

SUGGESTIONS—CHAPTER 4

1. Find three or four books originally published in the 1930s or 1940s and another three or four that were published in the 1980s. Which qualities found in the first group do you find in the second? Which are missing? Which qualities do you find in the more recent books that are absent from the earlier books?

2. Look at *Why the Sun and the Moon Live in the Sky* by Elphinstone Dayrell, illustrated by Blair Lent; *The Fool of the World and the Flying Ship* by Arthur Ransome, illustrated by Uri Shulevitz; and *Once a Mouse . . .* by Marcia Brown. All three books are Caldecott Medal winners. Analyze one of these books in detail.

3. If you have a serious interest in children's literature, you may find the books listed in Appendix III useful.

Part Two

DEVELOPING YOUR
IDEAS

*Like bees who by instinct go from flower to flower gathering
honey, writers, merely by being alive, are constantly
gathering ideas and impressions—their honey—which
eventually will lodge somewhere in some book. . . .*
  *—Eleanor Estes, from a talk given in New York to a meeting
      of the International Reading Association*

5

Where Did You Get That Idea?

WRITERS SEEM TO fall into two categories when it comes to ideas: those who are always looking for a good idea, and those who have so many ideas, they don't know which one to work on first.

Let's take the first group. These writers have good ideas, often, but forget or misplace them. The first rule, and the most crucial one, then, is to carry a notebook with you at all times. (This is the same one you started in Chapter 2 for jottings on observations and criticism.)

MAKING NOTES

Jot down ideas as they come to you, wherever that may happen—for characters, behavior, dialogue, titles, anything. Trusting that you will remember a good idea until you get home, to the office, or someplace where you can settle down, leads to about 99 percent loss of those ideas. Writing it down, even in hieroglyphic-like notes, at least calls it to mind and then you can fill in the rest. Use this notebook of thoughts, phrases, ideas for your future work.

I was walking along a busy street in midtown Manhattan when a drab little man passed by, carrying a large manila envelope. He was dressed all in nondescript colors from his head to his ankles, but on his feet were the brightest blue shoes I had ever seen. They caught my attention and held it so completely that it was worth a note, which I made on the spot and still have. I have no idea where or when, but someday, I am certain that the little man in bright blue shoes with the mysterious package will appear in a story or scene.

I know someone who had great ideas falling asleep each night but found she had lost them all by the time she awoke in the morning. She put a pencil by her bedside, and in the dark, without disturbing her thoughts, scribbled a few words in tiny script on the wall over her bed as the ideas came to her. It was fiendish on her walls, and she may have had to paint more often than most people, but she had the right idea about hanging on to those good ideas.

Let your notes run free, and use all forms of writing—dialogue, prose, verse, sayings, phrases—whatever helps you remember. Putting down these fragmentary reminders is a way, too, of training yourself to see in a new way, to be alert to all the possibilities around you, to cultivate your power of observation, your ability to absorb detail and store it.

Keeping a journal can be very useful to your writing as well as a fascinating personal experience. Just as the artist's sketchbook shows his growth from year to year, so will your journal show yours. At the same time, the events in your life will provide, in bits and pieces of real, everyday life, a resource from which you can draw when you need some very real, very human material to bolster your writing.

A Day At the Beach — Coney Is.?

Benny + Jo
Benny + Julie?
Charlie + Bo
Bo + Charlie

trolley
nets period?

Benny - tease
Sister - wants to
get even

A page of notes from my IDEAS file. Notice the reference to "A Day at the Beach" and the note "Benny is a tease—Bobby wants to get even." A story was germinating. The characters became Benny and a narrator (no name) in "A Day at Coney Island," published by Cricket *magazine in July 1976. Scribbled notes made in haste can work themselves into your subconscious and, eventually, into your work.*

Here are a few more exercises in observation:

1. Look for something new in the familiar. Perhaps it is the old vase Granny gave you seventeen years ago that sits on the mantle. Did you ever really look at the design painted on it? Did you know that she painted it herself? Perhaps she even made the vase. Whose initials are those on the bottom? Choose something that you see every day. Look at it more closely than usual. Maybe it's a spot in the front yard, or the porch chair out back, or the neighbor's dog.

2. Take a walk in your neighborhood. Look around you. Can you tell something about the people who live in the houses you pass from the color and style of their blinds or curtains? Look at the geranium perched on the windowsill; who do you suppose put it there? A young woman? An old woman? A person who misses a garden somewhere? Try to imagine what goes on behind one of the windows in your neighborhood.

3. Choose a room or a section of a room in your house; describe on paper exactly how that room looks, including every detail, without looking at it. Afterward, look at it again. What did you miss?

CLIPPINGS

Another way to urge ideas to the surface is to keep yourself open to all forms of communication, from news items and magazine articles to TV programs, cereal ads, overheard conversations, and theater posters. Clip photos and articles. Look for plot ideas, characters, mysteries, settings, colors, subjects for study and research.

Many writers create whole books out of small news items

that just give the most superficial details of a deeper story. In my files I have these: 2 KIDNAPPED CHILDREN FOUND SAFE ON COAST; ONE MISSING 7 YEARS; and RESEARCH IN HUMAN EM- BRYOS RAISES FEAR AND HOPE. They still fascinate me, so I won't throw them away. Others creep into the file, tempting, growing on me. You never know when one of these ideas will work its way out of the file and into your creative bloodstream.

Look closely at these everyday items or places in the next week or two. You will find ideas in some of them:

- bill stuffers
- posters
- ads
- TV news
- supermarket checkout line
- school cafeteria line
- parking lot
- fast-food restaurant
- locker room
- bulletin board
- laundromat
- playground

USING YOUR OWN EXPERIENCES

An extraordinary source of material comes from you, your- self. Explore your own feelings. These are the truest feelings you can write about because you know them intimately. Since you write about and for children, move back in time to when you were a child. Think back on how you felt, reacted to things; how you spoke, cried, thought. Remember your first day at a new school, the first time a certain boy or girl smiled at you; remember wearing a new pair of shoes, sharing something with someone you didn't like, a nasty grown-up, what your room smelled like, how a piece of bubblegum tasted, a game you invented with your best friend.

The apartment in Brooklyn in which I grew up is the background for one story of mine; in another I use Coney Island and the boardwalk, scenes of my own past, to underscore the atmosphere. One of my short stories involves a boy who has to take off some weight, a problem close to my heart, and a second takes place in a skating rink, tagging along with an older brother, again a situation right out of my past.

Go back into your childhood; put together scattered thoughts or memories until you have pieced together a whole episode. Go through a family album and try to remember what led up to the taking of each picture. What time of day was it? How did you feel about the other people in the picture? Where was the picture taken? How old were you? Where did you get the sweater or baseball cap you wore in that picture?

The more you work at piecing together the clues you see before you, the more you will evoke whole episodes and flavors and feelings of the time. Eventually, you will find yourself drawing on this personal treasury even when you are writing a contemporary story and the places in the photographs have ceased to exist.

BORROWING IDEAS FROM OTHERS

As you read more, try to see how the ideas for stories came to be. Read something about the authors; do a bit of research. You may also pick up ideas for yourself as you read about other people and their books. Within each story there are a dozen other stories floating around, waiting to be snatched up. A story about a foster child may remind you of a classmate you once had who lived with her grandmother; the grandmother may have been quite a colorful character in her own right. Could she be a figure in your next story? One thing does lead to another, and it can go on and on, this network of good ideas. Be open to it and willing to stretch a bit to look in all the corners; the possibilities are endless.

One way to meet the challenge of coming up with new material and new ideas in spite of all that has been done before is to take an old theme—a folktale, for example—and try to improve it, cultivate it, give it more depth and meaning. In doing this you will make it your own, and for the time being it will save you the trouble of coming up with a brand-new idea. Think of what Leonard Bernstein did when he took the theme from *Romeo and Juliet* and created the contemporary dramatic musical, *West Side Story*.

FOCUS ON ONE IDEA

Now let's see what happens if you are in that *other* group— the one where ideas come like grains of sand in a desert windstorm and settle thickly on the pages of your notebook. You probably have lots of unfinished pieces around, fat, bulging notebooks and files full of loose notes. In your case, you want to stop being just a notetaker and become a writer. You must focus.

Choose one of your ideas by any means at all. If one is particularly timely, you might choose it for that reason. Pick numbers from a hat if you cannot decide. Take that one idea and roll around in it and don't let it go until you can either feel the satisfaction of its completion or until you can safely tear it up and throw it away. This may seem harsh, but if you are stuck in the mire of too many unformed and unfinished ideas, you must do something aggressive to get out. Sometimes you simply have to face the fact that an idea is not as good as you thought it was and you should not waste more time on it. Most of the time this force of discipline results in a completed piece. Take the chance. However it turns out, it will start to unclutter your mind and your files. The feeling of accomplishment and freedom will enable you to move on to something else.

The important thing for the perpetual notetaker is to get something done, finished, to the point where you have devoted attention and time to it and have given it a fair chance. Many aborted stories are the result of too many ideas crowding in at once, preventing any one of them from having breathing space, a chance to survive.

Maybe you haven't got dozens of notebooks filled with half-done stories, but you've still got a problem with too many ideas; maybe all your ideas are still in your head. The same rule applies: *focus*. Get hold of your thoughts and put them on paper once and for all. Choose one idea, sketch it out. Don't labor over it; if you don't set out to do it perfectly, you will have a better chance at conquering your fears. Once the skeleton of the story is in place, you will find the courage to go on with it, to go back and put flesh on the bones.

Since your aim is to finish something, it is important when you choose a piece to work on that you choose something relatively easy, without complications. Avoid unnecessary barriers to success. Avoid, for example, a piece with a very unusual character or theme. If an animal is the main character, choose a familiar animal rather than a strange one. The only thing you want to stand out right now is your writing, and the trappings should not detract from that.

Whichever way you have to go to come up with an idea that works, remember that your ideas are worth writing about. It is in the telling that you compete, and that is where your skill as a writer comes in, sets you apart, makes the editor sit up and take notice.

SUGGESTIONS—CHAPTER 5

1. Choose a short period in one day when you are among a number of strangers, such as at the lunch counter, in a shop, riding on the bus, or waiting in the dentist's office. Single out one person and observe how he sits, walks, talks, moves, wears his hat or tie, how he carries his paper or pipe, and so on. Look at his hands. What can you tell from looking at them? Give this person a background, a personal history. What might his occupation be? His ethnic make-up? What kind of woman is he married to? What would he do if there were an emergency at the moment you are studying him? Make notes on the spot if you can and write up a character sketch later.

2. Clip an article from your readings in the next week that you think would make a good solid teenage story. Write a one-sentence plot outline for the story you would create based on this clipping.

3. Explore old folktales and find one that you would like to adapt for a picture book.

6

Sabotage Made Easy

I AM THE worst procrastinator the writing craft has ever known. No sooner do I sit down at my desk to work than I remember that my friend's father is recovering from bypass surgery so I should call to find out how he's doing, and that Aunt Lucy's 85th birthday is next week so I ought to run out and buy her a card right away so it reaches her in time for the big day.

If I am not careful and try to ignore these nagging ideas, the restlessness will build and finally I will get up from my chair. Maybe I will do some exercises. On the way to another room, I might notice that the fish need some food or that the light bulb in the living room needs changing (it went out a week ago Thursday) and think that maybe the dog hair problem wouldn't be such a problem if Kaspar had regular daily dog brushings, which I could start right now. And, while I'm interrupted anyway, I might as well call my friend who is home from work with a cold.

There is no end to the problems you can create to keep yourself from writing. Uri Shulevitz once called these games we play "sabotage," and I have never forgotten it. Sabotage it is, guaranteed to mess up your most perfect plan ... *if* you let it.

ESTABLISH PRIORITIES

It has very little to do with laziness or lack of interest and everything to do with fear—of filling that blank page with perfect prose; of meeting the expectations of friends, family, ourselves; of success (Can I handle it?); of failure (Why am I wasting my time?); fear that, at best, our work will be mediocre and, oh my, let us *never* be that!

The truth is, all writers have fears because all writers are human. With some, the fears get in the way of writing. Successful writers fear that they cannot top what they have already done and so they avoid trying. Unsuccessful writers fear that they are failures because they have not been published and feed that fear by avoiding more writing, perpetuating the failure-to-publish syndrome. *The words just won't be as crisp and as witty on paper as they are in my head. Maybe I have nothing really interesting to say. If I wait and think about it some more, I'm sure it will come out better.* There is always some excuse, waiting to be used. It takes courage to overcome fears, so start now training yourself in working up the courage you will need time and again to write. If you wait around, hoping that something will happen to get you back on the track, you are asking for defeat. Courage means pushing yourself into that first scary step toward where you want to go, not waiting for rescue.

There are ways to avoid playing this sabotage game, which you can never win. First, you must look at your writing in terms of priorities. How important is writing to you? Look clearly at how you view your interest so that you will know how much to demand of yourself for it. If writing is about as interesting and important to you as building a birdhouse for the backyard or cooking a gourmet meal, then don't put any more pressure on yourself than you would in those activities. Give writing the same time you do those things, and move at your own pace. Write for enjoyment, but don't think about publishing.

If writing is more important to you than anything—family, health, job—you are at the other extreme. You will not write to publish, either, but more to feed your passion, communicate with your muse, and you will not care if anyone else reads or likes what you write. If you are one of these writers, you should know that it will be difficult to maintain a family or social life while you write. Yours will be an eccentric situation, at best, and perhaps you ought to make some arrangements with your loved ones before you seal yourself off to work so that you can be reached in emergencies, have the children cared for, and so on. You probably won't have the patience to study methodically, but will surface to consult reference material from time to time.

If you are in between these two positions, you are the most likely to work out a system to incorporate writing into your life so that you can learn at a steady pace and have the time and space to grow as a writer. You must give writing at least the same attention that you would any on-the-job training program because that is what this is: training for your future as a writer. That means making room for it in your already busy schedule, for if you do not allow yourself the time and sense of importance, you will never become *any* kind of writer.

If you are worried that you may not be suited for children's writing, or that you won't be any good at it, relax. Give yourself the chance to find out, but do give yourself a chance. Only after you do the work and study and practice for a reasonable length of time will you be able to decide if writing is what you really want and have a good idea of your own abilities. Then, if you wish to spend more of your time and creative energy on your writing, you will have a better idea of what is required to accomplish your purpose.

Your life is 100 percent full now, so how do you make space for something new? Consider that you have made room before, for jogging or a computer course or meditation or doing your exercises in front of the tube. You know that you can always squeeze in 15 minutes a day, so start with that. Fifteen minutes should not turn your life upside down and can get you started on a very important course. Right now you are at the beginning of a brand-new discipline, and setting up regular work habits is far more important than the length of time you spend at it.

WRITE EVERY DAY

For the next two weeks, you must write for *at least* 15 minutes each day—and no days off, please. Those minutes must be good, fresh, energy-rich minutes, not "leftovers" from the day. Don't wait until eleven o'clock at night and try to cram in your writing before you go to bed. You are too tired then, and your head is too full of the day's activities and problems. Pick a fresh, uncluttered time. Perhaps it will be before everyone else gets up in the morning. Maybe you will find lunchtime, when the office or house is quiet and the phone is not ringing, the ideal time. If you must use the later part of the day, clear your head and lungs and get your blood full of oxygen by taking a walk or doing some deep breathing exercises before you begin to write. Any time that is truly yours will work fine.

When you sit down to write, write and *do nothing else.* Don't look for your lucky shirt or magic pencil; one day you will be without them and you will have to learn to write on your own, without lucky charms to help you. Write anything, as long as it is creative. Forget grocery lists, journal entries, and letters. Write stories or parts of stories, character sketches or bits of dialogue that you overheard on the bus yesterday; describe places, things, feelings. Try telling a story from the point of view of two different children or from an adult and a child's viewpoint, without using adjectives. Imagine yourself at age 7 going to sleep in a strange place and afraid of the dark, inventing ways to get your mom or your Aunt Lydia to come into your room. Think back on what it was like to have a grasshopper in your fist or a giant jawbreaker in your mouth, or what it felt like when your best friend found a new friend and left you out.

START TYPING

If you get the cold sweats as you face the blank paper on your desk, type out a few passages from a favorite book to get warmed up. (This is an excellent exercise, by the way; it gives you insights into other writers' use of structure and form.)

There are endless ways to use this time. You don't have to complete a story or even have a story idea ready each time you sit down. Bits and pieces add up and can be useful in later writings. They help you to observe the world around you. They are your sketchbook ... your training in observation.

If you think everything you write is junk and it depresses you to have it lying around, throw it away. Why torture yourself? This is practice, and you don't have to show your work to anyone. Toss things in the wastepaper basket, and remember to empty it at the end of the day. Leave no traces. Start fresh each day. Eventually, you will want to hang on to something, and then something else, and, as your confidence grows, so will your file of writings.

WRITE REGULARLY

As you do more writing, and can handle your 15 minutes with ease, you can stretch it to longer and longer periods. Be careful not to be overzealous and take on more than you can do, or you will defeat the purpose of the regular work habits. It is important to remember that regular periods of writing each day, no matter how short, are more important in the long run than spending several hours in a row at writing on weekends. Perhaps you will do both, but if you have to give up one, give up the weekend sessions and hang on to your daily discipline— at least for now. The weekend writer has to contend with revving himself up to the task each time, which can waste plenty of time. Your regular routine will get you so used to writing that eventually you will need only seconds to get in the swing when you sit down to work.

Sometimes the format of tidy chapters or sections creates its own set of problems for the writer. If you are writing a long book and have trouble with beginnings, try to resist the temptation to finish things off neatly each day. When you are sailing along smoothly, and all the major problems of a section have been worked out to your satisfaction, leave your work for the day. Don't wait to tie it up. Pick up on it the next time, when you can jump into the middle and continue right along with it, free of anxiety. Chances are once you have picked up momentum, you will go right into the next section as you finish the present one.

BUILD UP YOUR CONCENTRATION

Concentration is crucial when you write. It is important not only to maintain your thoughts but to keep you from wasting valuable time. If you have a problem concentrating, try to work out some of the simpler kinks. When you sit down to write, what are your main distractions? Is it too quiet? Try working with the radio playing softly in the background. Some writers find that classical music dulls other sounds and provides a relaxed atmosphere. The music you play should not be the kind that makes you hum or tap your foot or in any way interferes with your thinking.

Is it too noisy? Perhaps you need to work in some other place. Perhaps a friend will let you use her office or house during a part of the day when she is not there. Or try working at the library. Some have typing rooms or research desks for serious work.

Can you work by yourself or must you have other people around? Does it help to have your dog in the room or should you keep her outside while you work? Do you get stiff sitting too long at your typewriter? Get up from your chair every 20 minutes or so and do a few stretches; these are good for your back and neck, the main problem areas for writers.

Whatever the problems, identify them and work them out *before* you are ready to work, otherwise figuring out solutions becomes a distraction too.

After many years of giving in to sabotage, I have learned to work in my home successfully by exercising frequently near my desk and by keeping a thermos of coffee nearby so that I don't have the excuse of going out to the kitchen several times in one morning, I also have a telephone answering machine that is switched on during my working hours; it collects messages for me, and I deal with them when I have finished my writing for the day.

If after all these tricks you still suffer from distractions, you will have to work at building up your concentration, bit by bit. One way is to listen to a piece of music through to the end without falling asleep or dancing or doing anything else. Learn to listen, to identify the different musical instruments, to follow how the composer uses his theme throughout the work. Practice this for a while. Apply it also to reading. Read as many pages as you can in a book (for pleasure) before you are distracted or find yourself rereading whole passages. Time

---

EXERCISES FOR NECK AND SHOULDER STRAIN

1. Every 20 minutes or so, stand up at your desk. With your hands at your sides, raise and lower your shoulders ten times.

2. Keeping your hands at your sides, rotate your shoulders, first forward ten times, then backward.

3. Roll your head around as far as it will go, first to the left, then to the right. Repeat ten times in each direction.

Working for long periods over a desk or typewriter can put quite a strain on your neck and back. These simple exercises can ease some of the tension.

yourself. Aim for more pages in the same amount of time. Keep at this until you have built up your period of concentration to at least four times its previous length.

As you succeed in the music and reading exercises, work at improving your period of concentrating as you write. Refuse to get up from your desk until so much time has passed. Get tougher on yourself. Stretch out the period a little longer. As you increase your time, give yourself several days, or even weeks, to get used to the new time before pushing too hard for more.

Wear earplugs if they help.

GOOFING OFF

Once you have established how important writing is to you and have applied your interest to working out a time plan and a method of sticking to your work, *allow yourself plenty of goof-off time.*

This may seem counterproductive, but it is not. As a matter of fact, goofing off is essential to your success. It is how I learned to live with my propensity for sabotage, and you can learn it. You must have some time each day to make phone calls, jog, water the plants, read the stock market report, sharpen your pencils, get your shoes fixed, practice the piano, do a crossword puzzle, play with the cat, put a new tape in your Sony Walkman, play records, watch "M*A*S*H" reruns, or take a nap. Even if you do nothing in your goof-off time, take it anyway. If you don't have this outlet for the day-to-day "fillers" in your life, they will intrude at the worst possible time, your writing time, and interfere with your concentration.

Put a limit on this time. Goof-off time should not spill over into time allotted for anything else. Give it an hour, a morning, whatever you feel is reasonable, then stick to it. When you get to your writing, you will have only writing on your mind.

SUGGESTIONS—CHAPTER 6

1. Make a priorities list. Consider family responsibilities, social activities, volunteer work, chores, jobs, hobbies, schoolwork, sports, health, cultural pursuits. See where your writing fits in with the other things in your life.

2. Read Ezra Jack Keats's *The Snowy Day* (Viking, 1962). Type the text out in manuscript format. (See page 115.) Is it longer or shorter than you expected it to be? (Save the typed manuscript; you will need it for a later activity.)

3. Write a scene in a bus station with a young boy and an old woman. Base the characters on two people you observe during the course of this week.

7

Who Cares?

Sending manuscripts to publishers is a time-consuming business. It is not unusual for an author to wait three or four months for a publisher to return a manuscript with a form letter saying, "We regret that we cannot use your story at this time." No comment. No explanation.

At this rate, writers can grow old (not to mention crotchety) before they have a thing in print. Is there a way to cut down this waiting time? Is there some way to find out before you put in all the work and time if anyone is interested in your ideas? In some cases, yes.

THE QUERY LETTER

The query letter was designed to shortcut some of this long process and eliminate wasted time for both you and the publisher. The trouble is, it only works well with non-fiction.

Let's say that you are seriously interested in a topic—thunderstorms—for a book for 8- to 12-year-olds. Would publishers care about a book on this subject for this age group? Would they consider *you* capable of doing it? Is there any point in doing the lengthy research that will be necessary if no one would even want to read your manuscript?

First, look in a directory called *Subject Guide to Children's Books in Print* (found in most libraries and bookstores) under all the headings that would connect in some way to thunderstorms: thunderstorms, lightning, electricity, meteorology, weather, and so on. The Subject Guide will suggest other cross-references. Look for those titles that are marked for the age group for whom you will be writing. The school grades, rather than ages, are noted, so you would list in your query letter any that are for grades 3 through 7. For your later research, jot down adult book titles that could be helpful to you.

If you happen to choose an enormously popular subject like personal computers or whales, and you find dozens of books available for young people, you will have to ask yourself how you would make your book different enough from all the rest so that an editor would be willing to buy it and compete with the others for sales. If you can't come up with a terrific angle, you would be better off finding another topic.

From your previous study of publishers (Chapter 3), you should be able to make up a list of all the publishers who might be interested in your idea. Write to them asking if they would be interested in seeing your proposal or manuscript, if you have completed it. Note other books in print on your subject and for your age group and explain why your book would compete successfully with them. Of course, finding a publisher who has published a book on your subject means that you should *not* send your proposal there, unless the publisher is planning a series and your book would fit the series. The point of finding other books is to show the publisher to whom you are sending your work just what the competition is so he can evaluate your work in light of it. (If you don't, they'll look it up themselves, so do it and show them you're on the ball.) Explain why you find thunderstorms fascinating, and why you feel qualified to write the book. Include any publishing credits you may have that seem appropriate. (An article in your school paper is not; an article on energy-saving tips for a small magazine is.) Since you are unknown to them, you have to sell them on your subject rather than yourself. Tell them anything that might be persuasive in stirring up their interest, but avoid hard-sell tactics (This is the book you've been waiting for!) that will turn them off.

All of this should take no more than a one-page letter. The temptation will be to explain, to go on about your project and yourself, but don't—save it for another time. Right now, you are simply trying to interest an editor in the subject matter, to weed out those who have no interest whatsoever, saving you a great deal of time and expense. A query letter costs only the price of a first-class letter, but the larger proposal or manuscript costs far more, even at special manuscript rates.

It is perfectly human to want to tease, provoke, prod, and titillate an editor into being aware of your project, and I won't talk you out of it. If a childhood trauma involving a tornado spurred you on to write your manuscript, that could be just the thing to whet the appetite of the editor, even if it has nothing to do with the content of the book. Editors do like a bit of human interest, but keep in mind that the longer your letter goes on, the more you defeat your own purpose. The query should always be looked at as a time-saver for both sides.

As I said before, this only works well with non-fiction. Still, some publishers ask for queries regarding longer fiction and even picture books. While non-fiction is usually outlined carefully and a sample chapter will show the author's ability and

```
                         John P. Author
                         100 Lilac lane
                         Scuddy, VT  05148


Ms. Vera Blaine
Senior Editor
Children's Delight Publishing Co.
625 Riddle Street
New York, N. Y.  10025

Dear Ms. Blaine,

For the past five years I have been an animator at the
Merry Movie Film Company.  My work gives me insights
into the filmmaking process which I think could be
valuable in writing a book on the subject for young
people.

I propose my book for junior and high school students
who are making films for the first time.  To the best
of my knowledge, there are many books on filmmaking, some
of which include chapters on animation, but only two books
deal with this subject from the point of view of the
animator.  One was published in 1973 and is out of date
in light of recent production methods, and the other is
highly technical, for the adult.

If this subject is of interest to you, I would be glad
to send you a detailed proposal of my plan for the book.
A reply post card is enclosed for your convenience.

                         Sincerely,



                         John P. Author

Enclosure
```

*A query letter. Keep it brief and to the point for the best re-
sults. The reply postcard is tasteful and expeditious.*

style, fiction is often done without a written scheme and depends for its success on plotting, pacing, suspense, characterization, and other intangibles. A writer may have a good style and get off to a ripping start, but he can also lose his way halfway through a novel and never get back on the track.

For picture books, the query is even more difficult. True, the query process weeds out generic books such as ABCs and nursery rhymes, dictionaries, and counting books, as well as overdone themes like a visit to the doctor (dentist, orthodontist, physical therapist, psychologist) or a story about a child whose best friend has moved away.

The fact is, the shrinking of budgets and the resulting lack of staff and time have prompted publishers to ask for queries on just about everything. For longer fiction, give a brief synopsis of your story in a page or two. I usually recommend that for picture books, you simply send your completed manuscript—up to about six or seven pages.

When sending your query, enclose either a stamped self-addressed envelope or a self-addressed postcard that can be checked off and returned to you promptly. Once you have replies to your letters (allow three or four weeks for this) you will know those publishers to whom you will send your proposal or manuscript.

THE PROPOSAL

The proposal is a full presentation of the book that you have in mind. It sets up your plan for dealing with the topic in an organized manner and establishes your writing abilities and credentials to the satisfaction of the editor. It can be sent out as soon as you hear from a publisher—as a result of your query—that he is willing to consider it. Sometimes several months will go by between query and proposal, in which case you might mention that you are following up a positive response to a query made some time ago.

Picture books do not require a proposal from the writer. Illustrators who have picture book ideas should present a dummy book and samples, which is a form of proposal. This procedure is covered in detail in Chapter 14, "For the Writer Who Is Also an Illustrator."

For older fiction, it is wise to finish your manuscript before submitting it unless you are working on a long novel or are a very slow writer, in which case you can put out some feelers while you are writing the second half of your book. You may get some reaction or suggestion of possible interest, but no commitment. Except in the case of established writers, publishers will rarely offer a contract on fiction on the basis of sample material, no matter how good it is.

For non-fiction, it is possible to sell a book on the basis of a proposal. Your research need not be complete, but you must know enough about your subject to have a broad picture of it, to know how you will approach and handle your subject, and to be able to write in depth about at least one aspect of it. You will have to outline your material and complete one or two sample chapters.

If you send only one sample chapter with your outline, it should be from the middle of your book, not the first or last chapter. The first is usually an introduction to your subject, and the last is more or less a summary. Get into the heart of it; choose the part of the book that is most interesting for you and let that be your sample chapter. Your enthusiasm will be more constant and your writing will be at its best if you truly enjoy the material. If you send two chapters, one of them should be the first, introductory, chapter, and the second should be from the middle.

ABRACADABRA!

Creating Your Own Magic Show

From Beginning to End

CHAPTER I - <u>YOU, THE MAGNIFICENT</u>

This chapter deals with creating the image
of someone with special, magical, powers.
Adopting some sort of name, such as "Alan
the Amazing" or "The Mystifying Markwell."
Creating a costume to go with the image:
clown, formal, swami, wizard. Directions for
making simple costumes without sewing. What
it takes to convince an audience of your
magical abilities. Concentration. Self-
confidence. The need for good props.
Developing good practice habits. Having a
goal, like putting on a Magic Show.

CHAPTER II - <u>A MAGICIAN'S SECRETS</u>

In addition to regular, easy-to-come-by
props such as glasses, a plate, string, and a
deck of cards, and even some larger items
such as two chairs and a curtain, there are
props very special to a magician. These <u>look</u>
ordinary--envelopes, newspapers, cereal boxes--
but the magician has "treated" them so that he
may perform "magic" when using them. This
chapter goes into the careful preparation
of certain props which are needed for the
tricks in Chapter II. They can be made with
everyday objects found around the house.
Perhaps also a paragraph on why magic "works."

CHAPTER III - <u>YOUR BAG OF TRICKS</u>

The most fascinating types of magic tricks
described in detail. Step-by-step instructions
and illustrations. These ten tricks will form
the basis for the reader's magic show. Another
chapter deals with making the props for some
of these tricks. Each trick will have a
snappy title. Further reading suggestions
will be made, as there are a number of good
books on magic tricks and how to do them.
Tricks include: making something disappear;

sawing someone in half; changing one
thing into another; pulling something out
of the air; guessing something using ESP;
having something put itself back together
after breaking or ripping it apart; an
escape trick; a card trick; pushing one
solid object through another solid object.

CHAPTER IV - <u>PRESENTING...YOUR MAGIC SHOW!</u>

Once tricks are practiced and mastered,
props are in good working order, costume and
image have been worked out, and reader is
ready to perform in front of an audience, he
or she will need some pointers. First, there
is publicity. Sample tickets are shown,
which the reader can make himself. A word
about advertising, including posters. How
to attract an audience. Starting with a few
people and building up to larger groups.
Sample routines and programs for all occasions.
Suggestions for accompanying music. Having
an assistant. Staging and sets. A monogram,
or signature, of the "star." A grand finale.

*A sample proposal. This was for a magic book and had to
compete with lots of others still in print. I had to come up
with something unusual. Mixing magic tricks and showman-
ship seemed to work. The editor bought the project.*

In a covering letter give an overall view of the book and your credentials. You do not have to be an expert on the topic, but if there is any special connection between you and your subject, mention it. When presenting a book of mathematical puzzles and pastimes, it can help, if you are a high school math teacher, to say so. Similarly, a book on the natural history of the raccoon by someone who has spent the last four years as a country veterinarian can be important, so let the editor know about your position of insight and experience.

If you have special resources at your disposal to research your subject from a closer or more unusual angle than other books on the subject, that too is good to include when submitting a proposal.

Tell the editor the age group for which you intend the book and why your particular approach is going to make a difference. If you have chosen your subject well, then you are enthusiastic about it; let that enthusiasm come through. It's catching. The editor will feel it, and that can work in your favor. There is nothing as appealing as an author who is excited about his work.

Avoid writing about subjects simply because they are "in" or there is a "need" for them; you will only add to the dross in publishers' offices, the hundreds of unpublishable manuscripts, pedantic and dull, that come in from people who believe that researching a subject is enough.

You can send proposals and query letters to several publishers at the same time. If you have an offer from one of them during this period, it is courteous to inform the others.

The proposal shown on pp. 60–61 resulted in a contract. It is for *Abracadabra—Creating Your Own Magic Show from Beginning to End*, a long, detailed plan of how a book on magic would be organized into four basic parts, featuring creating an image, learning magic tricks, making and using props, and putting on a show. The first part (a fourth of the book) was sent with the proposal. Author Ross Olney uses a more streamlined version of a proposal that is short and to the point. It grabs the reader's interest with its snappy style and gives a thorough picture of the book in a single page. Why the difference? When I submitted my magic book proposal, I had never done a non-fiction book before and was an unknown quantity to the publisher, so I had a lot to prove. Ross Olney, on the other hand, can shortcut this procedure because he has published many books and a publisher knows from his past work how he writes and how successful his books are.

In all your mailings, remember the SASE, or self-addressed stamped envelope. It should become second nature to enclose one whenever you send anything to a publisher; query letter, proposal, inquiry, or manuscript. As a writer, you will need plenty of these, so you may want to prepare a good supply of them in advance . . . and hope that one day one of them will come back to you with an offer of a contract inside.

SUGGESTIONS—CHAPTER 7

1. Write a query letter. Choose one of the hypothetical subjects below as though it were your own idea.

   a. Searching for dinosaurs; non-fiction, 8–12
   b. Looking for your first job; non-fiction, 12 up
   c. A voyage on a whaling ship; fiction, 8–12
   d. Teenage romance; fiction, 12 up
   e. A boy who trains elephants; fiction or non-fiction picture book

Go back over the information and samples in this chapter and see if your letter is appropriate for the length and type of book that you are proposing. Don't forget to check the competition.

2. To whom will you send your query? List the six publishers most likely to publish your book.

Part Three

WRITING YOUR BOOK

I think, I dream writing, and writing is who I am. How much time I spend at it, who I write for, why I wrote and what next I will write, fall in the realm of propaganda. The fact is that I must write and writing is work, hard and exacting. . . .

—*Virginia Hamilton, from "Portrait of the Author as a Working Writer,"* Elementary English, *April 1971*

8

Learning Your Craft

·HOW CAN I develop an interesting style?
How do I know what age reader I am writing for?
Is my work any good if I have to keep revising it over and over again?
Is there a way to have my manuscript looked at professionally *before* I send it to a publisher?
As you get deeper into the work of being a writer, these and many other questions will fill your head. Some will be answered as you continue to write, and as you read. Let the questions motivate you and guide you, not intimidate you. They show your natural curiosity and your need to find out more about this field that is still so new to you.

DEVELOPING STYLE

It is not unusual for first attempts at writing to be unclear, unformed, too dramatic, or not dramatic enough. Stories may be too light to make into books with substance. Trust that this happens to everybody and that, as you write, your ability to use the written language and your ability to tell a story with the proper balance grows . . . and your style begins to emerge.

Style is not noticeable at first. Your very earliest attempts at writing probably show nothing but an eagerness to put words on paper, to communicate. Soon your personal way of seeing things begins to come through, and your particular facility with handling words and phrases, constructing sentences and paragraphs, gives your writing a mark of individuality.

You can improve your style as you go, but you cannot make it happen or watch it too closely. It is like watching your feet when you're learning to walk; if you watch to see how it's done, you stumble and fall. It has to happen naturally and easily. Once you are walking, however, there is nothing to stop you from adding a swagger, a hip swing, or a long stride to give your walk more individual character or flair.

AVOID CLUTTER

Concentrate instead on putting your ideas, clearly, on paper. Make the writing as lively as you can, but keep your language simple and clear, avoiding devices like flashbacks and changes of viewpoint until you are more experienced. Avoid anything that will clutter your story.

You will probably have some idea about whether your book will be appropriate for very young children or for 8- to 12-year-olds, or for teenagers, and that general idea is all that you need. You need not consciously write for a particular age group; believe it or not, your readers will find you. The age and behavior of the characters, the language you use, the story line itself will imply an age, even if it is not specified. Publishers impose an age tag on a book after it is written, mainly for cataloging and selling purposes. "I need a book for a 6-year-old," says a grandmother to a bookstore clerk who may or may not know all the books in the store by content. To help out the clerk, the publisher puts an age code on the flap of most children's books which is easily broken by the bookstore salesperson. Your average 9-year-old can also figure it out. The tag "04207" translates to ages 4 to 7, for example; "8/10; 3/5" means ages 8 to 10 or grades 3 to 5.

Your ability to revise and rework a piece shows your maturity as a writer. A writer's perceptions are constantly changing and reshaping; you can see something a third time around that escaped you totally before. Editors often see more clearly than the writer who is close to his work, and they can point out areas for improvement. If you are rigid about your work, unwilling to change words and sentences and paragraphs, you may be sacrificing the total book for the sake of some well-crafted words.

LEARN TO CRITICIZE YOUR WORK

Learning to be self-critical also happens along the way, but sometimes you need to come out of your writing cave to seek the help of others who have a professional eye or the ability to see your work more critically than you can.

There are manuscript critique groups, usually made up of a group of writers in a small geographic area, which meet on a regular basis just to read their work for criticism. Freelance editors will consult with you privately and read and evaluate your manuscript for a fee. You can find a listing of freelance editorial services in *Literary Market Place* (Appendix IV).

There are writing schools and courses of study in creative

writing, many of them at colleges and universities across the country. These will demand much of you, in terms of both time and productivity, but if you are ready for them, they can be very helpful. You may want to get more into the habit of writing and get your feet wet before you join a creative writing course, but it can be instrumental in helping you to understand the subtleties of form and structure.

If you know of an editor whose work and opinion you admire, try writing to that person requesting a private consultation, if it is available, or a recommendation of another editor who might do private manuscript readings and evaluations. Many editors have their hands full with their everyday work load, but a staff editor may be interested in picking up occasional "outside" work. Agree in advance about the fee to be charged and be sure you understand what the evaluation consists of. A reading and general overall report is worth less than a complex evaluation with specific line-by-line comments and follow-up readings after revision.

As you learn about your strengths and weaknesses, the trick is to work *with* the criticism you receive, and not struggle against it. You may not always agree with what you hear, but do pay attention: you may hear, above and beyond specific details, some larger truths that are important for you to evaluate. For example, if there is a question about the motivation of your main character, maybe your character is not drawn deeply or clearly enough; if there are problems with the story, perhaps there is a weakness in plot. It is important that you communicate exactly what you mean: if there is any confusion, examine the work for problems.

Eventually, you will be able to apply some self-critical questions based on the criticism you hear from others to your next work. This is one certain way to avoid the serious mistake made by so many beginners—sending out material to publishers before it is good enough to publish.

SUGGESTIONS—CHAPTER 8

1. Look around for writers' groups in your area. Start in the most likely places—adult education programs, colleges or universities, the local library or bookstore. If you cannot find one, how would you go about starting one?

2. Find an editor or editorial service that you think would be right for your picture book story (hypothetical). What criteria did you use for choosing?

3. A list of books on writing, in general and for children in particular, can be found in Appendix VI. Perhaps you can locate one or more of these books in your local bookstore or library. Each book will offer different insights into the craft of writing, even if many of the books overlap in general information.

9

Writing Picture Books

THE BOOKS THAT look the easiest to write—picture books—are, by far, the most difficult to write. Why? Because they depend on so few words to say so much.

A writer with endless words at his disposal finds it easier to get a thought across than, say, someone who is limited to one or two sentences. A novel can have 50,000 words and more; a picture book may be only one hundred fifty words long. Those words must be well written, well chosen. Who was it who wrote to a friend, "Sorry this letter is so long; I didn't have time to make it shorter"? If you have ever written poetry, you can understand a bit better the difficulty of containing large thoughts in small spaces.

The average picture book story is 1,000 words long, or four typewritten, double-spaced pages. Exceptions prevail, from zero words (no text at all) to 10,000 words (or forty pages).

FIND THE PAGE-TURNING POINTS

Because of the concentrated form, there is a knack you must develop for moving the story along at appropriate "page-turning" points. A good rule is that there should be no more words on a page than are necessary for the time needed to examine the picture. Picture books move along something like short films and, even if you are not an artist, you have to think visually to understand how they work. Just as the filmmaker keeps your interest by changing the scene continually, by varying the camera angles and distance from the subject, and by the time spent on each scene, so you as the "director" of your story have to remember to move things along. You need to know when you have stayed too long in one spot or with the same characters, when to introduce action or humor, when to build suspense, when to peak, and when to decline. A helpful exercise in understanding this flow is to make up a dummy for your picture book.

A DUMMY BOOK

The dummy book can be helpful to you in visualizing your story and in working out the flow from page to page. Make your dummy from folded typewriter paper and paste in the typewritten text, breaking it up wherever you think it is appropriate. This is only to help you, not to send to the editor. (See the standard designer's layout for a thirty-two-page picture book on page 74.) Remember to allow room for the title page, copyright notice, and dedication.

This all takes a good eye and ear and a superb sense of timing, so don't worry if you don't have it under your belt in one try. Seeing the dummy book with your words pasted in

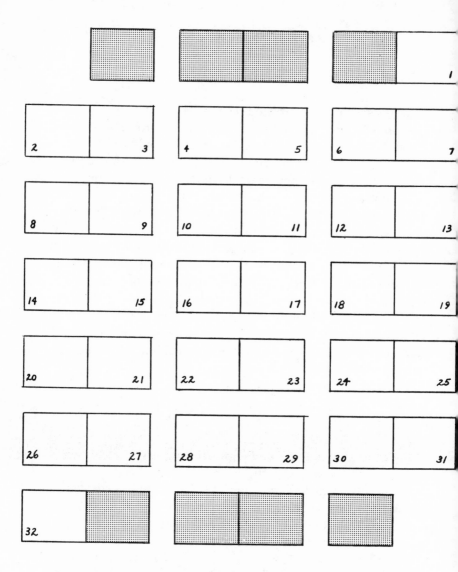

Layout for a thirty-two-page picture book. If endpapers are added (shaded area), it can become a forty-page book, utilizing all thirty-two pages for text and illustrations. The first, second, last, and next-to-last shaded pages are pasted down to the book cover.

place will move you along more quickly to understanding the limitations of space that you must learn in writing picture books. Nowhere will you see more clearly the excesses in your writing.

READ GOOD PICTURE BOOKS

Reading good picture book texts is one of the best ways to find out what makes one work. Read William Steig and Beatrix Potter, Jean de Brunhoff and Rosemary Wells, Margaret Wise Brown and Charlotte Zolotow, Jan Wahl and Russell Hoban. Listen to the language. Read the stories aloud and hear how the sounds trickle down to the ear. Be a child. Listen. Open up your imagination to what the words can do for you. "Children," Claudia Lewis reminds us in her book, *Writing for Young Children*, "are not to be thought of as any less receptive than adults to language that is art as well as communication. Primarily they want what we all want when we open a book— words that can work a little magic, a language strong enough to hold emotion."

Assume intelligence on the part of your reader. Don't be afraid to use big words or interesting words if they seem right for your story. Words beyond the child's immediate understanding stretch his mind and his vocabulary. Letting the sounds roll around in his mind and on his tongue will help him learn how delightful the use of words can be to express ideas.

THE STORY MUST STAND ON ITS OWN

A picture book story must be substantial enough to warrant a book of its own *regardless of the illustrations*. This is very important. Many writers of picture book texts rely, even unconsciously, on what the illustrations will do to bring out the intentions of the author. Your story must stand on its own. Text is almost always purchased separately from art. Illustrations are done later, by someone hired by the editor. The exception to this is when the author is also an artist, or a team has conceived an idea for which art and text cannot be separated. If you are not an artist, you are not expected to provide pictures with your manuscript. (If you are an illustrator, see Chapter 14.)

Books for very young children can be anything eye- or ear-catching: nursery rhymes; simple stories, tales or fables; nonsense verse; wordless stories to follow in pictures; simple word books to show concepts (counting, opposites, shapes, and so on); colorful books to introduce letters (ABCs) and words (BABY . . . BALL . . . CAT . . . SHOE . . .); repetitive and cumulative delights (*The House That Jack Built, Chicken Little, Old Mac Donald Had a Farm*). The full-fledged story, generously imbued with humor and drama, comes a little later as the child's attention and experience grow.

PARTICIPATION BOOKS

Participation books are important for the very young reader, who becomes involved by answering questions, acting something out, finding something in the pictures, or coming up with solutions to problems. Good examples of this kind of book are *But Where Is the Green Parrot?* by Wanda and Thomas Zacharias, a story with a built-in game of trying to locate the parrot in each picture, and *One Dancing Drum* by Gail Kredenser, which involves the child in counting musicians and their instruments as they arrive to play in the band.

There are no rules about what you should or should not write, but some themes are more in tune with the current market than others. With few exceptions, stories about inanimate objects are rarely successful. Sometimes, as in Hardy Gramatky's *Little Toot,* it works, but it forces the writer to exaggerate emotions to make the object more real, and the result can be too sentimental. Slim stories about desperately wanting something beyond reach ("A Pony for Jennifer") or doing something extraordinary ("The Boy Who Could Jump over Buildings") are done to death and should be avoided. Come up with a fresh approach if you are going to write picture books; even though there are only a handful of basic plots upon which all literature is based, your way of seeing things, your unique artistic vision, will make your story fresh and exciting.

THE DIFFICULTIES OF VERSE

There is a belief that editors do not like picture books in rhyme. This probably springs from the fact that hundreds of such manuscripts, poorly done, arrive on editors' desks each year. Writers who have not mastered prose fall back sometimes on forced rhyme and doggerel to help them through telling their stories. These crutches are obvious to the professional eye, and in some cases editors may have made blanket statements about not accepting verse in an effort to discourage further unskilled attempts from taking up so much staff time in reading and evaluating.

In your browsings, search out books with texts in verse. Dr. Seuss tells his stories in rhyme; so did Ludwig Bemelmans in his "Madeleine" stories. In spite of these and a few other exceptions, you will find very few successful books in verse. This difficult form is not easy for even the most talented writers.

If you write stories in verse and are not sure where you fit—

skilled or unskilled—be your own critic. Write the same story in prose until it is clear and satisfying. If you find that you fall into verse easily but cannot write without difficulty in prose, chances are you need to work on your writing skills more before attempting verse. When you can do either with equal ease and then make a choice to use verse over prose to tell a particular story, that's a different matter. Write in the form that is both comfortable for you and appropriate to your material.

ANIMALS WHO TALK

Another belief is that editors won't buy stories about animal characters who talk. This is not entirely true. James C. Giblin, editor of Clarion Books, was once speaking to a group of writers at a conference about fantasy and the imagination. A woman raised her hand timidly and asked, "Mr. Giblin, how do *you* feel about talking animals?" Jim thought a moment and replied, "Well, it depends on what they have to say." That's the truth of it. The fact is, if characters are drawn convincingly, and you have them in a good, solid, well-plotted story, there is no problem.

KEEP THE PLOT SIMPLE

A simple, clear plot is necessary for a successful story book. Even if there are several characters, focus on one and have all things happen from his point of view. Then have this character, your protagonist, be the one who comes up with a solution to your plot problem.

READ YOUR STORY ALOUD

When you have your story written, read it back, out loud. Use a tape recorder if you have one so you can listen to it. If you haven't got one, ask a friend or a member of your family to read your story back to you. Author Sue Alexander found this procedure so valuable that, if her family members were not available, she would prevail upon passersby to come in to read her work out loud to her.

Listen to the story carefully. Have you given the characters life? Is there suspense? Is the dialogue believable? Were there silent spots where nothing happened and you could "feel" the pause? Did you grab the listener's attention and hold it? Have your words helped the story progress? Did you move your reader in some way? If you use the tape recorder, play the story three times in a row. Parents and people who work with children must read the same books over and over to small children, who delight in repetition. Your story must bear up under this severe test or some crazed parent will feed it to the neighborhood dog when the children are napping.

Make every word count. Consider each one as costly—worth ten dollars, let's say. Can you save sixty dollars in that last paragraph? One hundred dollars? Two hundred dollars?

JUMP RIGHT IN

Start your story immediately. Grab the child's interest. Which beginning do you think works better?

Chadwick was a brown-and-white speckled dog.

Chadwick was lost.

The second line will perk up a lot more ears than the first. The vital word is "lost;" it is dramatic and pulls our interest right away. Your small reader will not wait for you to set up your story and describe your characters. If it doesn't get off the ground right away, he will simply pick up another book. So get right to it, jump in, take the plunge.

BE HOPEFUL

No matter what the subject (and none are taboo in these enlightened times), hopelessness does not suit this age group. This does not mean that you should sugarcoat the facts, but you should be sensitive to the emotional capabilities of young children. No matter what has passed, hold out to the child some possibility for something better. Give him something to help him cope as he struggles with difficult concepts.

One of our finest writers for young people, Katherine Paterson, writes in her book, *Gates of Excellence:* "I cannot, will not, withhold from my young readers the harsh realities of human hunger and suffering and loss, but neither will I neglect to plant that stubborn seed of hope that has enabled our race to outlast wars and famines and the destruction of death."

Where the Wild Things Are would not be the same book if Max had not found his dinner waiting for him, still warm, when he came home to his room. In Judith Viorst's *Alexander and the Terrible, Horrible, No Good, Very Bad Day*, Alexander just can't get anything to go right and nothing happens in the book to change that, but his mother, at the end, comforts him with the thought that some days are just like that, "even in Australia." There is a certain justice and comfort in knowing that people at the far end of the world are having just as horrible a day, and Alexander is not alone. One feels that he will wake up in the morning with hope for a better day.

CHECKLIST—PICTURE BOOKS

1. *A simple, clear plot is necessary,* if you write a storybook.
2. *Your main character must solve the plot problem.*
3. *Be visual.* Think of your story as a short film and keep things moving and interesting. Make a dummy.
4. *Read the best picture book writers.* Study their style, language, content.
5. *Use interesting language.* Never condescend to simplistic language. Talk up to the reader, not down.
6. *Do not find an illustrator for your story.* This is neither expected nor desired. Rely only on your story, not the pictures that will accompany it.
7. *Write fresh, new stories.* Avoid imitations and overdone themes.
8. *Read your story out loud.* Listen for its weak spots and how it bears up under repeated readings.
9. *Make every word count.* The average picture book is 1,000 words or four typewritten pages. With so few words, they must be chosen carefully.
10. Jump right in. Start your story immediately.
11. *End on a positive note.*

SUGGESTIONS—CHAPTER 9

1. Cut up the manuscript of Ezra Jack Keats's *A Snowy Day* that you saved from the exercise at the end of Chapter 6. Make a dummy book using folded typewriter or sketch-

book paper, pasting the text in place as you think it would work best. Don't look at the book until you have dummied the text to your satisfaction; then compare your version to the Keats version.

2. Write a story in 150 words or less. Make it a whole, complete story, with plot, characters, and so on. Do not use verse for this exercise.

10

Writing Easy Readers

HAVE YOU EVER looked closely at an easy reader? Almost every major publishing company has a line of these books now, and there is a pattern running through all of them.

They are illustrated, but they are far from being picture books. Their appearance is usually similar to older books. The size and shape are not whimsical; this "older" look is a planned part of the package. A child who has learned to read feels that he is no longer a baby. No matter that he still secretly picks up his old picture books when nobody is looking, to enjoy once again the familiar pictures and love-worn pages; in front of his older brothers and sisters and friends at school, he is reading, and that puts him in the category of a "big boy." His books, then, must reflect this pride; they cannot look babyish.

Inside the book, you will find further concessions to the new reader—large type, spacious leading (rhymes with *wedding;* the space between the lines of type), and ragged (uneven) right margins to avoid a heavy block-of-type look. There are fewer words per line, and fewer lines per page. Texts are often broken up into sections, or chapters; some even have a table of contents. An average easy reader is from 1,000 to 1,500 words long, usually in a sixty-four-page book.

As a writer, you should keep in mind that easy readers have been wrought with care and conviction for this very important reader. The nuances of their success are worth examining.

AVOID THE TEXTBOOK SMELL

You may think that, since easy readers are for children who are just beginning to read on their own, they are made up of words chosen from a selected word list, but this is not true. The great success of these books is that they do *not* use a controlled vocabulary and are genuinely compelling books with appealing design and interesting content. Some of the words may never have been seen or "mastered" before. Children are young, but they are not stupid; they can smell a textbook a block away. No wonder they love easy readers! They sense that grown-ups are giving them credit for their own curiosity and intelligence.

There are books that do use the controlled vocabulary approach, but tbey are more for institutional use than for pleasure reading. Used in the teaching of reading skills, some of them are very successful. Still, there is a difference between a teaching tool and a book for enrichment and pleasure. A child given a chance to read on his own will come to the book with a different attitude and expectations than one who is given "assignment" reading for development of skills.

If you feel that you want to write a book for the easy reader category, write it simply and forget word lists. The language should be rich and interesting. The sound and quality of the words and phrases are important, otherwise you can end up with a See-Jane-run blandness. When you introduce a word that you think is a challenge for the reader, use it again. Once the child has mastered the word, it is useful for him to be able to use it several more times until it becomes familiar.

Keep your sentences grammatically uncomplicated. Use simple, rather than complex, sentences, and avoid punctuation that elongates thoughts and ideas. Short sentences are easier for the beginner to handle.

The plot must be simple, uncluttered, and develop along clear lines. The resolution, brought about by the hero of the story, must be satisfying to the reader. Arnold Lobel's *Frog and Toad* books are examples of a break in this tradition, where both characters share equally in the "hero" role. Generally, there is one clear main character.

Children love humor—funny characters, funny situations. At the very least, be lighthearted if your material permits. See the humor in your situations and your characters. See any of Arnold Lobel's books for the best easy reader humor around. It looks so easy on the page, but Lobel confesses that writing, for him, is agonizing. He struggles harder with two sentences in an easy reader than with all the illustrations in the book. Perhaps this is because he sees himself as, primarily, an illustrator, for whom words come with difficulty. He has mastered the form, however, and captivates readers with his charming stories.

KEEP IT MOVING

Use dialogue whenever you can. Keep it short and snappy. The look of the text on the page is an important factor in easy readers. Lots of white space is a good thing, and dialogue helps to create white space. It gives life to the page.

As in picture books, think in terms of moving your story

along. Action is important; if your characters stand still too long, the reader gets restless. Have them do something interesting. Extraneous detail should be avoided; "describe" your characters through their behavior and dialogue.

Lillian Hoban, popular author and illustrator, says that you should create a single action in each sentence of an easy reader. Bette Boegehold, creator of several easy readers about charming Pippa Mouse, structures each sentence to contain an emotional idea. You get the picture. Pack it in, but keep it moving.

CHECKLIST—EASY READERS

1. *Write simply,* but *not* with a word list.
2. *The language should be rich and interesting.* Don't talk down to the reader.
3. *Keep sentences short.* Simple, rather than complex, sentences are best.
4. *Break up your story.* Use parts or chapters to divide the text into sections.
5. *Repetition of some words is often helpful* to the beginning reader.
6. *Keep the plot simple.* Focus on a single, uncomplicated problem in a clear story line.
7. *Humor is important.* Children appreciate funny stories.
8. *Use dialogue often.* The look of the text on the page is important; lots of white space is good.
9. *Action is important.* Avoid unnecessary detail that slows it down.
10. *Length is 1,000 to 1,500 words for an average easy reader.* The large type is set fewer words to the line and fewer lines to the page than in a standard book.

SUGGESTIONS—CHAPTER 10

1. Try to tell the story of *Little Red Riding Hood* in easy reader form. Make a dummy book and pencil in the text as you envision it on the pages.

2. Look at easy readers from different publishing houses. Compare the "package" of the total book against its competitors. Which do you think are the most effective, given your understanding of the genre?

11

Writing Non-fiction

IF YOU HAVE never thought about writing factual books
rather than fiction, you might consider it as a good way to
begin. It is one area in which your status as a novice has no
place in the consideration of a good work. If you come up with
a good idea and a fresh approach and show that you can handle
it successfully in your preliminary research and your proposal
and sample material, your chances of "breaking in" could be
significantly improved. Expository writing is easier to handle
for most beginners, and once you have your outline in order,
you cannot go too far astray, as you can with novels.

Young people like their information straight; they want material with which to explore and discover for themselves. It is
not necessary to fictionalize the facts. This does not mean that
you should not include a good story or anecdote in your text or
dramatize an interesting incident, for all of these things help to
enliven a subject and make a complicated piece of information
easier to absorb and remember. Once you choose and under-

stand a subject about which you care deeply, distill and simplify the information to explain it in terms that the reader will understand. The amount of distillation depends on the age and experience level of the reader. A few well-chosen details will be enough for an 8-year-old, for example, who wants a simple and direct explanation. For a teenager, you write at the interest and comprehension level of the average adult, which means that you can get into some pretty sophisticated concepts and terms as long as you avoid technical jargon and unnecessary details.

EXAMINE NON-FICTION

Look at the non-fiction work of Millicent Selsam and Seymour Simon, Barbara Brenner and Franklyn M. Branley, Joan Lexau and Isaac Asimov; these authors write lively books covering every possible age group, and they do it without leaning on fiction because their books are jam-packed with thoroughly fascinating information that needs no artificial support to capture the reader's interest.

As usual, there is an exception to the rule. For a good example of a fictionalized account of factual material, see Barbara Brenner's *On the Trail with Mr. Audubon.* In her research for the book on Audubon, Brenner found that a young assistant accompanied the naturalist on some of his trips to sketch the birds that they found. Her imagination took over and she told the story from the point of view of the boy, which she felt was more appealing to junior high school-age readers than an account of the naturalist in a straight biography. Another fine example of a skillful fictionalized account of true events can be found in the work of F. N. Monjo, who tells the story of a dramatic figure in history (Lincoln, Benjamin Franklin) through the eyes of a young person who spent some time around the famous person.

A GOOD TITLE

Never underestimate the importance of a good title for your book. Seymour Simon, well-known author of many fine books for young readers, recalls a book he published called *Chemistry in the Kitchen*. The book was good and was reviewed well, but in about a year, Vicki Cobb came out with a book called *Science Experiments You Can Eat*. The book was similar to Simon's, but became a runaway success. One can easily conclude that the funny, imaginative, eye-catching title of the Cobb book gave it the edge. With my own books, I know from letters that I receive that the zany titles of my "little-known facts" series are often the reason why readers pick them up in the first place. There seems to be something irresistible about a title like *You Can't Eat Peanuts in Church and Other Little-Known Laws* or *You Can't Show Kids in Underwear and Other Little-Known Facts about TV*. For the younger reader, a more straightforward title may work better. *My Puppy Is Born* by Joanna Cole and *Alligators* by Evelyn Shaw tell the young reader exactly what to expect when he picks up one of these books.

WHERE TO RESEARCH

Since successful non-fiction depends on the proper presentation of ideas and thorough research, I recommend that you study carefully the section on queries and proposals in Chapter 7. Also look into research techniques and resources beyond the

For a book that is highly dependent on graphic material (excluding traditional picture books), it is a good idea to make a thumbnail layout of your book, sketching in roughly how you envision the book. This can help you in working out text problems by realizing how much weight will be placed on text, how much on graphics. You don't have to be an artist to do this, since it is just a working tool. This page is from a layout of a sixty-four-page puzzle book.

usual. Make it your business to find out what materials are available on your subject and then go after them. Be creative. The library is certain to have the materials for a good beginning, but it can be only a beginning, depending on how much deeper you want to go into your subject. Consider the time you have to do it in, what you are being paid for the book, and how much information you will need before you can attack your subject intelligently, and come up with a workable plan. You will probably have your approach figured out by the time you finish the research for your basic proposal.

With a bit of probing, you will find private organizations with special materials on your subject, people who can be interviewed about their role in some area of development, experts who can answer specific questions that have not been answered satisfactorily in books.

When you are dealing in facts, your sources must be impeccable. Responsible researchers verify their information by means of cross-checking with two or three reliable sources, or by having the top person or people in the field look at their manuscript. In some cases a publisher will pay an honorarium to a noted specialist to read your manuscript for accuracy.

I remember calling the American Museum of Natural History once to confirm my findings about the odd migration pattern of the monarch butterfly, which affected exactly one sentence in a book I was then working on. I spoke to the chairman of the Department of Etymology, a charming gentleman who was delighted to talk to me about monarchs and proceeded to give me much more material than I could ever hope to use. He was all the more helpful when he understood that I was writing for children. Scholars, in their infinite wisdom, have considerable respect for passing on accurate information to young people.

There is so much fascinating information waiting for you that it will be hard to stop; you will probably overresearch your book. That isn't a bad thing; you need at least three times as much material as you will use anyway. It is important to have a big cushion of additional information so you can continually select intelligently what you put in your book.

If you are under contract, don't deviate significantly from your outline without first checking with your editor. When you are heading for that deadline and the research keeps on going, you will simply have to call a halt to it and stop taking in new information.

KEEP GOOD RECORDS

The records you keep as you dig should reflect all the important sources that you have used. You may need them later, for anything from compiling a bibliography for the book to answering fan letters after the book is published. Also, keep clear information and credit lines for pictures and quoted material that you want to use. Whenever you use a book or file or newspaper, take down the name of it and all its reference numbers—issues, volume, date, whatever. Also note page numbers and existing credit lines. This will save you the trouble of going back to these same sources later, which is time-consuming and sometimes even impossible.

If you want to use more than the 50–200 words generally accepted as "fair use" from a written work that is protected by copyright, you may have to get permission to use them. Lines of poetry and song lyrics are viewed more protectively than most prose so this rule of thumb will not apply. Your publisher may help you by giving you its judgment on fair use or by providing the proper forms, but you will probably have to write for the permission yourself. Your contract spells out who is responsible for permission fees, so be sure to discuss this at the time you sign the contract.

The average length of a non-fiction book for 8- to 12-year-olds is about 25,000 to 30,000 words. For older readers, 12 and up, 30,000 to 40,000 words is about right.

CHECKLIST—NON-FICTION

1. *Choose a subject you care about.* Your enthusiasm should not wane during the researching and writing period.
2. *Length for ages 8 to 12 averages 25,000 to 30,000 words. For teenagers, average book length is more like 30,000 to 40,000 words.*
3. *Look up the subject in Subject Guide to Children's Books in Print.* Note the competition.
4. *Send a query letter.* Ask if there is interest in your topic.
5. *Send a proposal.* To those who respond favorably to your query, send an outline, a sample chapter, and a letter of intent.
6. *Send your best sample chapter.* Choose a chapter you enjoy working on from the middle of your book.
7. *Verify your information.* Cross-check with two or three reliable sources.
8. *Go to the experts.* Ask top people in the field your questions or ask if they will look at your manuscript.
9. *Overresearch.* Do at least three times as much digging as you will actually need for your book.
10. *Follow your outline.* If you deviate from your plan, let your editor know.
11. *Keep clear records.* These are helpful later for permissions, answering editors' queries, preparing bibliographies, and so on.
12. *Tell it straight.* Distill and simplify to meet the needs of your audience in giving information and explaining facts, but do *not* fictionalize to "lighten" your material.

SUGGESTIONS—CHAPTER 11

1. Choose a subject that you know you would like to explore. Do a total of two hours' research on it, and write a proposal for either a "middle-age" or a teenage book.

2. To do a book on weather experiments for 8- to 12-year-olds, where would you go to find information?

3. If you plan to write non-fiction, an extremely helpful resource is *Finding Facts Fast* by Alden Todd. See Appendix IV for details.

12

Writing Novels

WRITING A NOVEL is an intimate, exasperating, exhilarating, perplexing, immensely satisfying experience, with something new to learn at every turn. At the heart of it is a good story, but then there is more. How do you tell the story? Through which character's eyes? Against what background? How do you keep your reader with you, turning pages to find out what happens next? How do you juggle humor and suspense and believable incidents and dramatic scenes and still have a clear plot and all its necessary subplots?

These are not all the points to watch for in writing a novel, but if you pay attention to these most important elements, you will find the course a lot smoother and avoid many problems that come along naturally when working in this form.

PLOT

E. M. Forster explained the difference between story and plot this way:

The king died and the queen died. That's a simple story.

The king died and the queen died of grief. That's a plot.

Before you do anything else, write down a one-sentence description of your novel. Difficult to do? Then you have a plot problem.

The plot should be crystal clear in your mind or you will end up trying to plug holes and fix leaks that become more and more difficult the more you plug and fix. A story can move along and characters be amusing or lifelike without a plot. I know. I've done it. You get very nice comments from editors about the funny dialogue and the appealing characters, and in spite of all that, the manuscript is turned down because the editor didn't know what it was about.

If you start off with a vague plot idea it can go awry; you lose focus, take too many unmanageable turns. One way to stay on the track is to write an outline of your story before you begin. Remember that your plot is your plan of action, how your story moves from point A to point B and then to point C. The plot answers the question: "What is your book about?"

Be sure that your plot problem is appropriate to the interest level of your readers. Your main character must be the one to solve the problem, or your story will fall flat. Nobody wants to stick with a person all through a story, sympathize with him, suffer with him, and then have someone else waltz away with the credit for tying up the problems of the book. Work to make your plot convincing; don't use corny gimmicks and obvious devices to get yourself into and out of interesting situations. It is better to have more ordinary events done in a believable way than to stretch your credibility in an effort to be clever.

A good novel should have several story threads that contribute to the main plot, but the reader should not be aware of them; they must be woven invisibly into the story.

Readers from 8 to 12 like clearly defined plots with lots of suspense, humor, and action. Atmosphere and high drama are not lost on this group. Read Paul Fleischman's *The Half-A-Moon Inn* for a story that fits this description perfectly. Less atmospheric and more thoughful, Betsy Byars also reaches the heart of this age group, as does Katherine Paterson.

Teenagers can handle more complex plotting. They are ready to deal with ideas and like to probe beneath the surface of things. They want humor, too, but at this age it's a wackier sort. Stories often deal with personal relationships and the shaping of ideals. Read the provocative novels of Robert Cormier, M. E. Kerr, and Paul Zindel for the best examples of this genre.

SUBJECT MATTER

You've heard the old saying "Write about what you know." Reaching for exotic people and places for your stories may symbolize the freedom of a writer, choosing any subject, letting your mind wander freely. This sometimes works for the seasoned writer, but the reality is that it is quite a handful to take on an unfamiliar world and make it convincing to the reader, even for most experienced writers. Characters seem to be cut out of cardboard; locations are as fake as movie sets; plots are farfetched or confusing. When you are starting out, take hold of things and people and feelings you can reach out and touch; they are what you know best, and you can make them come alive. Maybe your childhood was not glamorous or exciting, but you can still feel the cold coming through the hole in your mitten as you walked to school on winter mornings, and you can taste the simple home-baked cake that Mama put in your lunch box each day. You can recall the fluttery stomach you had on the day you had to stand in front of the class and recite a poem. This is what you should write about.

CHARACTERIZATION

As a beginner, you should use no more than four characters in your novel. Too many characters without real purpose can cause confusion and spread your reader's interest too thin, so keep the number to a minimum. If you have more than four, only give names to the most important ones.

You can come up with full, rich, flesh-and-blood characters if you know them well enough. To do that, keep a file, a character profile, on each person who will appear in your story. Include his name, family background, school history, medical history, relatives and friends, his favorite color, TV program, and arcade game. What was his favorite toy when he was little? How does he feel about math? Girls? School? What does he do in his spare time? *What makes him tick?* in other words. Your secondary characters need profiles just as much as your protagonist but perhaps in less detail. These studies should enable you to show characters accurately in any situation. Show us their faults as well as their virtues, but draw us to your main character with a balance in favor of his virtues. Give the reader an understanding of your characters' motivations, what makes them do what they do, so readers can identify with their hopes, their successes, their feelings.

BACKGROUND

Just as you round out your characters, you will have to create an authentic background for your book. This is the structural support on which your story will be built. The background can reflect the style and family history of your characters; it can be the church or religion that is mentioned here and there; it is the street and the house and the room and the way the furniture is arranged in that room. It is how people talk, which reflects not only their geographic location but their education and their attitudes. Sometimes you will have to do a great deal of research to be accurate; if you write about a hockey player with a moral dilemma, as Alice Bach did in *The Meat in the Sandwich*, you'd better get out there and learn the game. If your story is about survival in the outdoors, as was Jean George's *The Other Side of the Mountain*, you'd better know something about the outdoor life, as George does.

Even when you write fantasy, you must do it convincingly, grounding it in the familiar. Sometimes, a few well-chosen words will swiftly transport you from the real world into the make-believe. "Once upon a time" is one phrase that works such magic; another is "Long ago and far away." For futuristic novels, you must find ways to take your reader into the fantasy world and keep his or her belief suspended for the whole time that you are there. To do this, you will find that using commonplace details of life as we know it in this time and place, transfigured into comparable details in a future century, works the appropriate wonders. Today, we speak; tomorrow, we may transmit thoughts electronically . . . but the common denominator is that we are "talking" to one another.

BEGINNING AND ENDING

As an editor, I found that many new writers actually began their stories on the first page of Chapter 2. With the physical descriptions of characters and places left behind in Chapter 1, they felt free to move ahead with their story, and that is when the interesting part began.

Look at your manuscript. When does it begin to grab the reader's interest? Examine the first lines of several children's novels and see how different authors start their books. Rarely will you find physical descriptions of characters or settings. That kind of basic information is woven into the text as the story progresses; it is wasteful to spend a whole chapter or a section of a chapter on it.

Now look at your ending . . . have you gone on too long? This is like the previous problem, but at the end of the book rather than at the beginning. Feeling the need to wrap things up and "explain" yourself, you may have gone on past your natural ending. Trust your reader and yourself. If you have not made your intentions clear by now, a final wrap-up is not the solution, and it will be obvious—and boring—to the reader. Scrutinize your last paragraph, page, and chapter. Are they really necessary?

THEME

People are sometimes driven by their own strong personal experiences to tell their stories and to use fiction as a way to reach people. The idea is that, while the reader is being entertained, she can also be warned or persuaded or educated. Rarely do these stories break through into popular acceptance, unless the author has enough talent to pull the material away from the didactic approach and make it something more than a sermon. Avoid writing "message" books; they are much too difficult to do successfully (with the message hidden enough to be palatable).

Every book has its theme, of course, but that is a different matter. The theme is the writer's topic, and his personal point of view on that topic is bound to come through. It is different from plot, which is what happens in your story. For example, in L. Frank Baum's *The Wizard of Oz*, the theme would be, "Be it ever so humble, there's no place like home." The plot, on the other hand, would be how Dorothy gets herself out of trouble and home again after a tornado drops her in the fantastical world of Oz.

Choose a theme that is appropriate to the age of the reader. Teenagers are struggling with ideals and values, and for this reason themes on moral courage frequently appear in their books, even when the books are romances. Stories should be perceptive of the sensitivities and changes in a teenager's life and offer insights into how one might cope with an overwhelming need for justice, principles, values in a less than perfect world.

ACTION

Young readers of all ages want plenty of action in their books, not necessarily the cops-and-robbers or car chase variety, but *movement*, involvement, a sense of something happening. More sophisticated readers can coast along for a while on crisp dialogue and intellectual ideas, on intricacies of plot and character development, but even with the advanced reader, you can't keep things quiet for too long. The reader wants to be involved, feel that things are moving ahead, alive.

Sometimes the lack of action, or the feeling that there is no action, can be traced to a problem that seems to grab hold of beginning writers. It is the compulsion to *tell* the reader what's happening, instead of *showing* him. Editors often scribble "SDT" in the margins of manuscripts, standing for "show, don't tell," which shows you just how common a problem it is.

Here is an example of a scene from *Cinderella* to illustrate the difference between telling and showing.

Telling

At the stroke of midnight, Cinderella left the Prince and ran from the ballroom, down the stairs to the coach below. One of her slippers fell off but there was no time to pick it up. She got in and the coach took off, arriving home just as the last chime of the clock rang, and everything turned back to the way it was before.

Showing

Bong.
Midnight! Where had the time gone?
"I must go," said Cinderella, breaking away from the Prince.
"Wait! Stop!" cried the Prince, running after her.
Cinderella turned to look.
Bong.
She picked up her dress and dashed down the steps. In her hurry one of the glass slippers fell off. There was no time to stop and pick it up.
Bong.
The coach was waiting. She jumped in quickly.
"Hurry!" she cried.
The coach raced through the night. At the last stroke of midnight it turned into a pumpkin and Cinderella was no longer in the gown but in her familiar rags.

VIEWPOINT

When you are in doubt about the viewpoint, consider the difficulties of working in the first person. ("I was a perfectly normal guy until Brenda entered my life. . . .") Many teenage novels and quite a number of younger ones feature the first person viewpoint because it is personal, even intimate, and gives the reader the feeling that he really knows the narrator. Some editors feel it is just right for teenagers; others say they are tired of it, as are readers.

A viewpoint should not be considered because it is fashionable, but because it works or does not work for the kind of book you want to write.

With the first person, you have to speak more as people actually do . . . you can hardly avoid a heavy use of idiom. You never get away from the narrator's position; you see the world through his eyes only; you can't see what Brenda is doing three blocks away or how the team is getting on without him. You have to stay "inside" your character at all times, and that can get very difficult, especially when you're in the thick of your story and could use a chance to get away from your main character for a while to observe him. You cannot do that if you are using the first person and can only see through his eyes. Your narrator would have to be a rather dull, ordinary person who can see the main character and events objectively for the purposes of the story . . . he cannot be too strong a figure himself, or he will impose his personality on the protagonist and take something away from him.

With a third-person narrative ("Sam walked over to Brenda and smiled sheepishly. . . ."), you, as author, can see more of what's going on; you can position yourself wherever you need to be to move your story along. You also know what someone else sees or thinks or feels, not just your main character. You can move back and forth between two characters and give us broader insights into the story development from various angles. Many writers choose the third person but maintain a single viewpoint, which seems to be a blend of first and third person. This is less intimate but still highly personal; you step out of the narrator's shoes but you still stick close to him. In other words, you are not in his skin anymore, but you still see everything from his viewpoint, a single focus.

DETAIL

For very young children, actions speak much more effectively than descriptive details. Look at some of Beverly Cleary's books, particularly the ones featuring Ribsy, Henry Huggins's dog. He is a living, breathing, slurping dog, and yet he is barely described. We know him by following him around, watching him sniff garbage and bark at a fish and follow Henry around, wagging his exuberant tail.

Details in older books tend to help create atmosphere, but if they are implanted correctly they do not intrude on the reader. Descriptive information about characters and settings should be woven into the action, the real storytelling, and only if it is important. To say that a girl has pigtails is obtrusive. To say that a girl's pigtails flew out behind her as she raced down the street gives you a bonus... that same information plus action that tells you more about your character.

CONFLICT

There is no real story unless there is some conflict. If Cinderella had no conditions to meet on the night of the ball, there would be no story. Sure, everyone would have danced happily ever after, but there would be no *story* in it. Conflict adds layers to your story that give it more substance, more understanding of human nature. Decisions and problem solving come with the job of novel writer; they are not easy and should not be presented as easy to your reader: struggling through something gives a certain satisfaction to anyone.

Jimmy wanted a catcher's mitt and got one. See? There's no story there.

Jimmy wanted a catcher's mitt to show the other kids at the game. He could save for it, but that would take months, and the game was next week. He had to do something fast, but what? Stealing was out . . . or was it? He knew if he went to Jason's after school he could hide a mitt under his jacket and never be caught. The salesmen were friendly and always too busy to notice him.

Aha. Now there's a story: many layers of story, depending on Jimmy's choices.

DIALOGUE

Dialogue should have a point. When your characters speak, what they say and how they say it should show us character or background that would be otherwise difficult to explain. Dialogue should also help to move your story along.

S. E. Hinton's kids are tough city kids, and you know this as soon as they open their mouths. Vera and Bill Cleaver have drawn young people with remarkable inner strength and conviction; you know this when they speak.

You will have to develop an ear for speech that can be absorbed, distilled, and put on paper without losing the quality that makes it real. Listen to the way young people speak to you, to their parents and teachers, and to each other: those are three different things. Listen to girls speaking to girls, girls speaking to boys, boys speaking to boys. Of course, this makes an eavesdropper out of you, but it's for a good cause. You want characters who speak as real people do, in a manner appropriate for the age, the speakers, and the place.

What makes accurate dialogue is not speech as it would be recorded on tape, but speech that helps to define your characters, that sounds like the people you write about. Why are the two not the same? A novel shot through with dialogue such as this would be laughed at.

> "Jeet?"
> "No, joo?"
> "Nah, no time."
> "Where ya goin'?"
> "Jill's. Wanna come?"
> "Nah."
> " 'Kay. 'Bye."
> "See ya."

It would soon be boring, as well as difficult to follow. "Yeah" and "dunno" and other actual sounds made by most young people in their shortcut speech look and sound wrong when set in print. It's up to you to figure out how to capture the feeling of young people talking, usually moving and excited, without losing that spontaneous quality. Read Beverly Clearly, Paula Danziger, and M. E. Kerr; find out how these authors handle dialogue. No two have done it the same way, and all are successful at it.

Use the word "said" in dialogue, rather than a substitute like "growled" or "shouted." "Said" is considered an invisible word to writers, hardly noticeable to the reader and, therefore, invaluable because it does not get in the way of the action. Cut out all the "buts," "thens," "therefores," and "howevers" and you'll learn to rely on substance instead of transitions.

SUSPENSE

Telling the reader everything up front is a sure way to kill suspense. Every story can benefit from its author holding back enough so that the reader remains eager to find out what's going to happen. You don't need a cliff-hanger to do this, just a certain amount of tension necessary to maintain interest. Use characters to create suspense through a quarrel or a discussion or some action shaped by them.

TITLES

Titles can give away too much too soon, also. You know everything turns out all right in something called "The Answer to Heather's Wish." The best titles give you a dramatic notion of what the book is about but don't give much else. *Circle of Fire, Where the Lilies Bloom, Summer of My German Soldier, The Cat Ate My Gym Suit*—these are all good titles because they make us want to open the book and find out more. You can even pick the funny book out of the group by the title alone. Try to come up with a good title for your book. This is easier for some than for others, but is worth the effort. Many a book is chosen by a reader based on title alone.

LENGTH

A novel for the 8- to 12-year-old will run approximately 25,000 words. For older readers (12 and up), the average length is 40,000 words, although the actual range is more like 30,000 to 60,000 words. "Hi-lo" novels, which favor the disadvantaged older reader, are shorter, about 10,000 words in length, broken down into many chapters.

108

CHECKLIST—NOVELS

1. *The plot is your plan of action.* Sum it up in one sentence. If you can't do this, your plot is in trouble.
2. *Write about what you know.* You will write more convincingly if you stay away from unfamiliar subjects.
3. *Write a character profile on each person in your story.* These help to make flesh-and-blood characters.
4. *Your background must be authentic.* You can invent it, but it must be grounded in reality.
5. *Be sure your beginning and ending are where you think they are.* Did you wait too long to start? Did you go on too long at the end?
6. *The theme should be appropriate to the age and interest of your reader.* Avoid "message" stories.
7. *Show, don't tell.* Let the reader know what happens by showing him, in actions, not telling him about it.
8. *Viewpoint should be chosen with care.* With first person you are inside the narrator's skin; with third person you can observe more widely.
9. *Use details to create atmosphere or emphasize a story point,* but have them come out in the story gradually, unobtrusively.
10. *Conflict introduces the element of choice and adds dimension to your story.* Without it, you have no real story.
11. *Dialogue should sound right for the characters,* have a point, and help move the story along.
12. *Suspense adds necessary tension.* Don't give everything away right away; hold something back to keep the reader interested.
13. *Your title can help sell your book.* Choose one with care, hinting at what the book is about but not giving too much away.
14. *Manuscript length for 8- to 12-year-olds is approximately*

109

25,000 words, while those for readers 12 and up average 40,000 words.

SUGGESTIONS—CHAPTER 12

1. Write a character profile for the protagonist in a novel you want to write. Keep adding new information as you think of it.

2. Choose a first-person and a third-person book for teen-agers. Rewrite one page of text from each from a different point of view. Does the point of view change the feeling of the story radically? Which do you prefer? Why?

Part Four

SELLING YOUR BOOK

To sell stories, do three things:
1. *Study your markets.*
2. *Get manuscripts in the mail.*
3. *Keep them there.*
    —*Dwight V. Swain,* Techniques of the Selling Writer

13

Submitting Your Manuscript

IT IS AT this point that those ads in the writers' magazines stating "We are looking for writers like you" and "Let us publish your manuscript" begin to look appealing. Why go through all this bother and hard work? If you want your book in print so badly, why not go to one of these companies?

The publishers who run these ads are subsidy, or "vanity," publishers. For a fee, paid by you, they will print and bind your manuscript and deliver 5,000 copies (or some other prearranged amount) to your door. Does that mean your book is now published? Not really. Publishing is much more than printing and binding. Who will review your book? Many books will not be purchased without reviews to guide the purchasers. Who will distribute it? Those 5,000 copies will do you no good sitting in your garage. Lastly, who will buy your book? Maybe you can sell fifty copies to friends and relatives; then what? You have to let people know that your book exists, so you will have to advertise.

There have been some success stories with self-publishing and, after all, some of the most famous writers published their own works—Virginia Woolf, D. H. Lawrence, Thoreau—but look into the practice thoughtfully before you consider it for yourself. It may be right for your cherished book of poems or your family history, which may have only a small audience, but if you want your book to reach a wide readership, it is usually wiser to follow the traditional procedures and find ways to be creative in your writing instead of in your publishing.

When you feel that your work is the best it can be and you are ready to send it out to a publisher, you have reached an exciting point. In your eagerness, it is very easy to slip up on something important, such as forgetting to enclose a stamped self-addressed envelope or mentioning your publishing credits. These guidelines will help you to remember all those last-stage procedures.

TYPING YOUR MANUSCRIPT

Type your story on one side of the paper only. Use good quality nonerasable white bond paper, 8½ by 11 inches, at least 16-pound weight. (Heavy paper costs more but stands up under handling better and looks nicer. I use 16-pound for rough drafts, 20-pound for the final version.) Margins should be about 1½ inches at the bottom.

Number the pages of the manuscript (except for page one) consecutively throughout, not chapter by chapter. Type your name and address in the upper lefthand corner on page one. Type the title of your work halfway down the page, centered, in capital letters. Two lines below that, centered and in lower case, type the word "by." Two lines below that, type your name or pseudonym, centered and in upper and lower case. Double-space your text and indent for paragraphs. In the

```
Jane Smith                           (No. of words)
100 Pleasant Street
Middletown, MO  65201
```

```
                    TITLE OF STORY

                          by

                     Jane Smith


        This is how your manuscript should look when it is

    presented to an editor.  Your paper should be 8½ x 11

    white bond, preferably with some rag content, for dura-

    bility, and no lighter than 16-pound weight.  Be sure

    your typewriter keys are working and clean, and that

    your ribbon (black only) is fresh.  Leave margins on each

    side of about 1½ inches.

        Start your first page halfway down the page with the

    title, all in caps, centered.  Under that, type "by"

    (centered) and under that, type your name, in upper and
```

*This is standard manuscript format. After a while, you will
know how to do it without looking at this sample, but until
you do, use it whenever you prepare a manuscript for submission to a publisher.*

lower case. Type your complete name and address in the upper left corner and an approximate word count in the upper right. (There are about 250 words per full typed page.)

The first page is not numbered, but subsequent pages are, in the upper right corner. Your last name and a key word from the title should appear in the upper left. Text from page two on (except for chapter beginnings) begins about $1\frac{1}{4}$" from the top. Each new chapter begins on a new page, halfway down the page.

Type on one side of the paper only, double-spaced, and indenting 5 or 6 spaces for paragraphs. Keep a carbon or photocopy of the manuscript for your files and send the original to the publisher. Do not staple, clip, or bind the pages when submitting a manuscript.

You can fold a short manuscript (3 to 5 pages) in thirds and mail it in a #10 letter-size envelope. Longer manu-scripts should be mailed in manila envelopes with cardboard backing or, if they are very long, in a cardboard box (the one your typewriter paper came in is fine). Always include postage for the return of your manuscript.

Address your manuscript, with a brief covering letter, to a person, not just a department. On re-submitting a manuscript, retype the top pages if they are dirty or creased.

upper righthand corner, indicate the number of words (approximately) in your manuscript.

Identify the work with a title page that includes your name and address in the lower lefthand corner. This page also serves as protection; if it gets soiled and has to be retyped, it's not a big deal, but you don't want to have to retype the text. Your last name and a single word from your title should appear in the upper lefthand corner of the rest of the manuscript pages.

MAKING CORRECTIONS

Check your manuscript carefully for errors. If you cannot make corrections crisply and cleanly on the typewriter, do the page over. A few inked changes are all right, but more than a few will make your manuscript look sloppy.

ROUTING THE MANUSCRIPT

Keeping up with those trade publications and publishers' catalogs now begins to pay off. You should have a good sense of where you are going to send your manuscript. It should not take much brushing up to prepare a list of the five or six publishers most likely to respond favorably to it. If you are following up a query, the publishers who said they would look at your manuscript are already set out for you.

Make up a routing slip showing the title of your work, the publisher to whom you sent it, the date on which you mailed it, and, if you receive an acknowledgment, the date it was received at the publishing house. (If you want to be sure of an acknowledgment, send a postcard for this purpose, self-addressed and stamped, when you submit your manuscript.) Leave space for the date that you receive the manuscript back

```
TITLE: _____

  Description: _____
  Age: _____ Words: _____
  Proposal: _____ Partial Ms.: _____ Full Ms.: _____


ITINERARY:
                                    Date
    Publisher        Date Sent    Returned    Comments
  _____       _____    _____   _____
  _____       _____    _____   _____
  _____       _____    _____   _____
  _____       _____    _____   _____
  _____       _____    _____   _____
  _____       _____    _____   _____
  _____       _____    _____   _____
  _____       _____    _____   _____
  _____       _____    _____   _____
  _____       _____    _____   _____
  _____       _____    _____   _____


SALE:

  Date of Contract: _____ Publisher: _____
                                             _____
                                             _____
  Editor: _____ Art Director: _____
  Rights sold: _____
  Ms. Delivery Date: _____ Art Delivery Date: _____
  Copy/copies received: _____
  Subsidiary Sales:
  _____
  _____
  _____
  _____
```

This is a routing slip, but any form that works for you (index card, ledger, notebook) is fine if it provides at-a-glance information when you need it. This particular form shows my natural optimism, because it includes room for contract information.

Date_____

Dear Ms. Richards,

This hereby acknowledges receipt of your
manuscript, GREAT DAY IN THE MORNING.

Sincerely,

_____

CHILDREN'S DELIGHT PUBLISHING CO.

It will hurry things along for you and the publisher if you enclose a self-addressed stamped acknowledgment postcard along with your manuscript.

and any remarks or comments. Once a contract is offered, you may keep other records; this is just to show where your manuscript is at any time, and to keep track of who has seen it.

COVERING LETTER

Address a person, not a department, when sending a manuscript. A covering letter is not necessary, but if you want to send one, keep it brief. Never give a synopsis of your story or explain your work in a letter accompanying a manuscript; the work should explain itself. If it needs help, it isn't ready to be sent out.

Your covering letter should include the title of your work, any publishing credits, and reference to a previous query.

A listing of publishing houses and individual editors appears in *Literary Market Place* and other reference books and directories (see Appendix IV).

MAILING YOUR MANUSCRIPT

Picture book manuscripts should be typed on full pages, not as you visualize the final book, with only three or four lines to a page. Do not indicate illustration breaks; this is the editor's job.

Dummy books should only be sent by illustrators. The exception to this is when you are writing a piece for which the concept is not clear through text alone. A fine example of such a book is Ellen Raskin's *Nothing Ever Happens on My Block*. While a boy laments that nothing ever happens on his block, behind his back some very interesting things are going on. The book's success depends mainly on the visual "joke"—and would have to be noted in the manuscript. Show the editor what you have in mind with a rough dummy of the book. Use stick figures or blobs if necessary; your artistic ability is not a factor in this situation. A very simple but neat dummy can be made out of folded typewriter paper. Print in the text or use cut-up typewritten copy.

If your manuscript is less than four pages long, you can fold it in thirds and put it in a regular letter-sized (#10) envelope, but I prefer the small manila envelopes of 5 by 7 for picture book manuscripts. I feel that if I send a #10 envelope it may go astray, into the regular mail, instead of with the manuscripts, adding an unnecessary delay to my waiting time. If you use the manila envelope, fold the manuscript in half. Up to ten pages can fit neatly into this package. Anything longer should not be folded. Use a piece of cardboard to keep the pages from being bent or folded in transit.

For manuscripts more than 100 pages long, it is advisable to use a cardboard mailing box. These can be found in most stationery stores, or for really big manuscripts, you can use the box that your typewriter paper came in. The box protects the corners of your manuscript from becoming dog-eared in everyday handling and from rattling around in post offices and mail rooms. Retyping a manuscript is time-consuming and costly, and you want to invest in anything that will help you keep it looking fresh. The advent of word processing may be the answer to this problem. With your manuscript neatly filed on a disk, all you have to do for a clean copy on paper is to set it up to print (on a separate printer) a whole or partial manuscript or just the pages that need freshening.

Do not staple pages together or bind them in any way except with a simple paper clip.

Include a stamped self-addressed envelope with everything you send a publisher, from a query letter to a final manuscript.

If your manuscript is peculiar in shape, size, or bulk, have it sent to the publisher by special mail service, packaged with care, and with complete instructions and postage for its return. If you live near a publisher, you can arrange by phone to deliver and pick up the manuscript yourself.

It is not a good idea to send artwork with your manuscript. The text alone is what the editor wants to judge. Never have an outside artist do illustrations for your story. An editor will provide for illustrations if she buys your text. If you yourself are an illustrator or work closely with a collaborator, send along a couple of sketches and one piece of finished art, and the editor will look at these. It is still your text that is under consideration, however, and illustrations will not make up for what is lacking there. Many writers send out material before it is ready, but provide art for it; perhaps they feel more comfortable hiding behind pictures. The sad thing is that, if anything, it tends to put the text under closer scrutiny in the editor's effort to overcome any influence that the art may impose. The more appropriate method for showing illustrations, yours or someone else's, is to show samples of your work to an art director, independently of text. See Chapter 14 for details of this procedure.

POSTAGE

Postage requirements change from time to time; you should consult the domestic mail manual, available at all post offices, for current rates and rules. Mail clerks are not always knowledgeable about such things as manuscripts, so do the looking yourself. The current manuscript rate may change but, hopefully, there will always be some inexpensive way of sending original manuscripts through the mail. Perhaps this is another point for word processors and sending disks, rather than manuscripts, to publishers. Disks are about as lightweight as a letter. First-class mail is fastest, but it can be expensive after a few mailings, especially if your manuscript is a novel. Be sure the return envelope you enclose with your manuscript has sufficient return postage; manuscripts received without appropriate postage may not be returned.

WAITING FOR A DECISION

You will probably wait a long time for the publisher's decision. The time varies from house to house, and can be from three weeks to several months. Small houses with small staffs generally take a lot longer to make decisions than a large house with a lot of readers. After three months, you can follow up your submission with a query about whether your manuscript is still under consideration. A self-addressed postcard with pretyped responses is a help to the publisher and will bring you a quicker response. If a publisher still holds your manuscript, send a letter stating that you look forward to a decision by a certain date—say about a month from the date of the letter. If you do not hear from them by then, you will feel free to submit the manuscript elsewhere. Should you then have to send a copy of the manuscript to the next publisher, explain that the copy represents the original, otherwise it will appear to be a multiple submission.

MULTIPLE SUBMISSIONS

What is wrong with multiple submissions, or sending the same manuscript to several publishers at the same time? It is a matter of the traditional ethics of the business. Many publishers have softened their views on the practice because the waiting time for decisions has increased and poses a real hardship on authors.

The feeling against multiple submissions is understandable. From the publisher's point of view, it takes a great deal of time, effort, and money to read unsolicited manuscripts (those sent directly from author to publisher without benefit of agent or in response to an editor's request) and give them a fair evaluation. An editor does not want to feel that he is being pressured into a decision, nor does he want to invest his time and money—which comes out of his department budget—to consider a manuscript, send it to various readers, have reports made up, and then discover that someone else has bought it while he was considering it. Some editors refuse to read manuscripts submitted in this fashion and return them unread. Unless you have information from a good source that a house is willing to look at multiple submissions, send your work to one publisher at a time. (Note: Remember that this does not apply to queries and proposals, which can be sent out in quantity.)

If you decide that you wish to send out more than one copy of your manuscript despite this attitude, follow these rules to avoid disappointment:

1. Send multiple submissions only to publishers who are sympathetic to the practice. Marketing surveys (which are discussed in Chapter 15) will generally include this information.
2. Let the publisher know that it is a multiple submission.
3. Indicate a date, about three months from the date of submission, by which you would like a decision. Do not make a commitment until that date, and do not press anyone to make a decision before then.

AGENTS

You do not need an agent to sell your manuscript. A few publishing houses have announced that they can no longer afford to read unsolicited manuscripts, but the vast majority continue to read everything that comes in, looking for new talent. It is extremely important that you learn how to sell your own work and to present your material in a professional way. An agent can do no more for you until you get to the contract negotiation stage. Still, you may feel comfortable with an agent who can advise you all along the way. You will find a full listing of agents in *Literary Market Place*, and in the writers' annuals.

Be aware that some agents charge a reading fee; in some cases this is a legitimate part of the business, since it takes time and effort to read manuscripts, but in others it is a lure to new authors to pay a large reading fee without the follow-up interest of a true agent, to place your work with a publisher. One way to distinguish one from another is to ask for an agent's client list. See how many published authors an agent represents before committing yourself to an agency.

At the point where you are offered a book contract and feel that you need some professional advice, consider hiring a lawyer to read the contract for you and see that your rights are protected. Not every lawyer knows book contracts intimately, but they do understand legal documents and will look for anything that is a violation of rights, hidden or surprise clauses, and so forth. A lawyer will not cost as much as an agent, generally, since you pay a lawyer a one-time fee. With an agent, you pay a commission (the standard rate is from 10 to 15 percent of the advance and all future royalties on that book).

Experienced writers will tell you that they find agents either intolerable or invaluable; it's all in your personal relationship and expectations. Many writers prefer staying in control of their manuscript routing and editorial responses, preferring to have the agent step in only after a contract is offered. It is difficult for beginning writers to find agents, since most deal only with established authors. When you have several books published and no longer need to bother about establishing yourself as a professional, you may want to hire an agent to negotiate a more complex contract. Until then, try it on your own and learn your business well.

EDITORIAL COMMENTS

It sometimes happens that an editor will ask to see further work, even if the present submission cannot be used. Be sure to follow up on this; if you are fortunate enough to receive comments of any sort about your writing, even this indication that your style is interesting, you would be wasting a real opportunity to let it pass you by. If you should receive suggestions on how to revise your work, be sure to send the revised manuscript back to the editor who made the suggestions. Use every opportunity that comes your way. (There is more about this in Chapter 16.)

COPYRIGHT

I have never personally known of a case of anyone's idea being stolen in the process of submitting work to a publisher. Beginning writers seem to have a preoccupation with this notion and go to great lengths to protect their manuscripts. The fact is, you cannot copyright an idea ... and for good reason. Ideas are duplicated all the time. It is the execution of those ideas that makes a work unique. Think of all those Renaissance Madonnas, for example, and how many artists worked on the same theme, relentlessly, and yet no two are alike. Writers often come up with exciting and wonderful ideas only to find that someone else has already thought of them, or to learn that three publishers are coming out with books on the same subject in the next publishing season. There is not much to be done; duplication of ideas is bound to occur.

There is a relatively new copyright law, however, which protects your work from the moment it is in "fixed form." This means once you have your story in manuscript form, you are protected automatically. Your records, such as your routing record, should be sufficient evidence of the date of ownership. However, to be on the safe side, especially if you are a worrier (and some of my best friends are worriers), mail a copy of the manuscript to yourself, first-class or registered mail, and keep the sealed envelope in your file. *Do not open it,* even for a lawyer, unless it is before a judge and witnesses. This is known as a "poor man's copyright." Forms for official copyright may be obtained from the Library of Congress in Washington, D.C., but it is not necessary to apply for copyright yourself. Your publisher, on publication of your book, will do that for you, in your name. Note however that with magazine publication, copyright is generally taken in the name of the magazine, and you have to write requesting the reversion of rights after publication.

You are now taking a very important step in your journey into children's book publishing . . . and the hard part, the waiting, has yet to begin. There is only one way I know to make this time go easier, and that is to get going on your next project. Start a new book or story or article. Get completely involved with a whole new set of problems, characters, and situations. The time will pass a lot faster, and you will be less anxious about the work that is out. More important, you will prove that you are a writer by getting on with your work.

SUGGESTIONS—CHAPTER 13

1. Send to the Copyright Office, Library of Congress, Washington, DC 20559, for *free* booklets on copyright: #R1, "The Nuts and Bolts of Copyright," and #R99, "Highlights of the New Copyright Law," about changes in the copyright law since January 1, 1978.

2. Make up a loose-leaf notebook or an index file for your routing record. Use the format on page 118 or any that you find convenient.

14

For the Writer Who Is Also an Illustrator

ALTHOUGH THIS IS a book for the writer, there must be a chapter included for those of you who draw or paint as well as write, and whose artwork is inseparable from your writing.

To be a professional illustrator you must have the ability to handle the technical skills required, such as preparing a storyboard, making a dummy book, preparing color separations, drawing, and telling a story visually. An illustrator should have at least a familiarity with production techniques and have the ability to lay out a picture book in a balanced way, relating pictures to text in a smooth, interesting, and attractive fashion.

When you have both text and pictures for a proposed book, send the following to the children's book editor at the publishing house of your choice:

1. *A typed manuscript.* The manuscript should be typed and presented separately from the one you cut up to paste in your dummy. (See number 4 below.)

2. *One piece of finished art, in color.* The completed illustration should be representative of your style and ability. It can be in color, but keep in mind that book budgets do not often allow for full color, so your art should reflect that you are aware of this and are able to visualize illustrations in two or three colors or black and white. If you are asked to do the book, you will be expected to do it in preseparated art, which will be explained later.

3. *Sample sketches in black and white.* These sketches will give the editor an idea of your overall ability to draw and to show characters in action, your individual style, and your sense of the dramatic.

4. *A dummy book.* Make up a dummy in the size you feel is right for your book. Use drawing or visualizing paper for this, and attach a cover made of heavier paper or board. Pictures should be sketched loosely in place. Indicate where the text will go with ruled lines or typewriter copy. Work up a cover design for the book, in color. Although it does not have to be finished art, it should represent the book and show you at your best. The dummy shows your ability to design a picture book to flow from spread to spread with the proper rhythm and interest.

Remember to use the appropriate number of pages—thirty-two or forty-eight. Picture books are printed on both sides of a single press sheet. With careful cutting and folding, the sheet is turned into groups of folded pages, called signatures, which are later sewn together and bound. The picture book illustrator must lay out a book with this sheet in mind. A thirty-two- or forty-eight-page book can be made from this single press sheet, which keeps the price within the bounds of the average book buyer. Endpapers can be added separately at the time of binding so that all thirty-two or forty-eight pages can be used

JUST ME

Barbara Seuling

Today I am a dragon.
My face is scary.
my claws are very sharp

The cover and an interior double-page spread for the dummy of an easy-to-read book. Only after the editor approves it are galleys cut up and pasted in place. Until that point is reached, you can indicate where type will go by blocking out areas of type or ruling lines.

I can make fire come out
f my nose.

for text and art. Of course, you always have to allow for the title page, copyright notice, and whatever else the publisher wants to include.

Any medium or technique that can be reproduced on a printed page is suitable for children's books. Choose the one that is comfortable for you and that suits the type of book you are doing. Experiment. Ezra Jack Keats won a Caldecott Medal for his work in collage, *A Snowy Day*. Robert Quackenbush works on waxed rice paper for interesting texture. Don Bolognese and Elaine Raphael used woodcuts for their picture book *Turnabout*.

A cautionary note: paints do not reproduce as accurately as inks. Inks are absorbed into the paper and paints lie on top, which means they reflect light differently. A reproduction from inks is always more accurate to the eye. Printers can match inks to inks better than to paints for this reason. Permanent markers work fine but they tend to fade rather quickly; keep work done in markers out of strong light.

When an editor or art director hires you, you will be called in to discuss your plan for the book, your technique, your method of separation, and details that are important to the book, plus a time schedule.

THUMBNAIL SKETCHES OR STORYBOARD

The first step is usually for you to prepare thumbnail sketches or a storyboard, a rough plan of how you plan to lay out the book and distribute the illustrations. You make a storyboard by ruling the outlines of your pages on a large sheet of paper. Using the same colors you plan to use in the final pictures, sketch in very roughly what you will show in each picture and where the text will fit on the pages. The storyboard is discussed with the editor and art director before proceeding with full-sized sketches.

Sketches are worked out to show more detail, but they are loose, not finished drawings. Placement of elements and characterization are important at this stage. A dummy book is made up with the sketches in place. All color should be indicated at this time. The editor and art director go over it, this time for content, continuity, color, and logic. (If a boy has green socks on page three, he should have green socks on page five.) Typewritten copy should be pasted roughly in place. When the work gets final approval, you proceed with finished art. As galleys become available, you will be given a set which you can cut and paste on your mechanicals, or finished pieces of art.

COLOR SEPARATION

A word now about color separation. Each color in a piece of art to be reproduced must be photographed and made into a separate plate for the printing press. The plates are run separately, first for black ink, then yellow, then blue, then red. For fewer colors, there will be fewer plates and fewer times that the paper has to go through the press. The camera-separation process, done with filters, is costly. Therefore, the artist is asked to do the separating of colors.

Look in a children's book publisher's catalog. Books in color are described as two-color, three-color, or four-color. That tells you how many plates there were in making the book—usually how many separations the illustrator had to make for each piece of art.

When starting out, a simple and economical way of doing separations is to do a basic drawing, then drop in each flat area of color on successive acetate overlays. This is most commonly done with India ink or with sheets of stick-on color, available in art stores. The basic drawing is usually done in black with colors added afterward on progressive sheets—one for red, one for blue, and one for yellow. For a two-color book, you might have a basic black plate in line or halftone with one orange overlay for your second color. This overlay can be the same solid color throughout or broken up in percentages of color and mixed with the black, also in percentages. For example, if you were to lay a 40 percent orange overlay over a 20 percent black area, you would get a shade of brown in the final printing. If you placed it over a white space, you would get a light shade of orange.

The thing that is hard to fathom at the beginning is that this second color (or third, or fourth) overlay is done in black. (Some artists use red; it is even more intense than black.) The book dummy helps the illustrator in the separation process. There you have your colors worked out and approved before you begin. All you need to do now is translate the color in your dummy into percentages of blacks and grays on your overlays. It is your job to figure out just what percentage of each goes into the colors you want to achieve. For this, you will find invaluable a book of colored ink swatches broken down in percentages. You can buy one of these in an art supply store, or look at one in the art director's office. The art director may also help you get a color chart from the printer showing all the colors that can be made in various combinations and percentages.

Another method that is relatively simple for the inexperienced illustrator is waxy pencil (like china markers or Eagle Prismacolor pencils) on drafting film, which can be purchased in an art supply store that carries architects' supplies. The film is made of mylar and comes in various thicknesses—.003 or .004 is good for this work. One side of the film is matte and takes both waxy pencil and ink. You can see through the layers of film as you work.

Paper can also be used for overlays, but water-based inks or paints will cause the paper to curl and wrinkle. If you use nonbleed paper, you can use markers in percentages of gray for overlays of flat colors.

If you work on an opaque surface, you can use a light box, either a professional one or a homemade one. For many years I used a sheet of lucite propped up by a stack of books on either side. A fluorescent camper's lamp below let me see through the paper I was working on.

As you become more proficient in separating colors, move up to more sophisticated methods. It takes a great deal of patience, experience, and skill to do tonal work with paints or inks in color separation, but it is possible. Uri Shulevitz is a master at this process. Look at his book, *Dawn*. Watercolor paintings in gray and black washes were made to represent the brilliant emergence of the sun on the lake and mountains after an early morning watch by a child and a grandfather. In the printing process, his blacks and grays were transformed into brightly colored pages. Shulevitz says that he prefers separating his own colors, even when given the choice of separation or full-color painting, because he has more control over the final results and the colors come out cleaner and crisper. This is certainly evident in *Dawn*.

It is only fair to state once again that unless your artwork is of professional quality, send your manuscript *without* pictures. The demands upon even the most talented illustrator are great but can be handled with ease if you have mastered certain skills.

Many of the skills you need as an illustrator are learned in art school. Some, like color separation, may not be part of the curriculum unless illustration is featured. Occasional courses are offered in extension systems or adult education classes. A professional illustrator who lives nearby might be willing to tutor you in the basics of color separation or ink techniques or whatever you need to know. Once you have the essentials, you will learn by doing it.

STUDY OTHER ILLUSTRATORS

In addition to the traditional methods of training, study the works of other illustrators, past and present, not to copy them but to learn from them. Note their use of color, form, detail, and space. See how they solved the various problems of technique and story. Find an illustrator who has made excellent use of two or three colors and another who wasted his opportunity. See how flat, decorative treatment works in some books but not in others. Notice the attention to detail in books on nature subjects for young children. There is much you can learn from the experienced illustrators. If you are not fortunate enough to have one nearby for one-on-one training, use books to guide you through the insecurities of starting out in this exciting area. A list of books on the subject will be found in Appendix VIII.

If you feel that you are a better writer than illustrator, continue to show your manuscripts to editors and, separately, take a portfolio of your artwork around to art directors, or mail your samples, if you live out of town. Keep the two apart for now, until you are equally confident in your writing and illustrating abilities. While you are learning about illustrating books, perhaps you may pick up a job doing book jackets or spot drawings.

Finally, as the illustrator of the book, you will probably receive a share of the royalties depending on your contribution to the whole book. These rates vary, but on picture books you almost always share fifty-fifty with the author. If you do both text and illustrations you will probably not get much more of an advance than the writer alone would receive, although some publishers increase the amount. The best part is knowing that you will get to keep the entire royalty of 10 percent.

SUGGESTIONS—CHAPTER 14

1. Prepare a storyboard for a familiar folktale, such as the *Three Little Pigs* or *Jack and the Beanstalk*. Make it for a thirty-two-page book in three colors.

2. After you have prepared a storyboard to your liking, carry it a step further to making up a dummy book. Type out the story and cut it up to paste on the pages of the dummy where you think type should be placed. Make a cover for your dummy. You can use this in your portfolio if it looks good, so take your time and do it with care.

3. An organization you might want to know about is the Graphic Artists Guild at 30 East 20th Street, Room 405, New York, NY 10003, tel. 212-777-7353. Membership includes legal and accounting referrals and a professional hotline, where you are put in touch with people working in the graphic arts if you call with a problem.

15

Marketing Strategies

MARKETS ARE CHANGING—expanding, contracting, reshaping—all the time. Within a year, the emphasis can shift from one kind of publishing to another. This happened in the 1960s, when Dell brought the paperback revolution to the children's field. It happened again in the 1980s, when it appeared that the traditional market for children's books—the library—was not as dependable as it once was, due to cuts in book budgets and personnel during an economic recession. All of a sudden there was a glut of very commercial books on the market, available in bookstores, where the publishers hoped to make up for their library losses. There were pop-ups and foldouts, activity books and whole lines of teen romances, books for which you could choose your own ending, and books that talked.

Finding the right home for your manuscript takes a great deal of skill . . . at least if you want to find it in your lifetime. According to current indications, it takes approximately four months for the average manuscript to come back from a book publisher. Some publishers take six months to a year to make a decision.

LEARN THE MARKET WELL

It is possible, however, with an effort on your part, to learn about the shifting marketplace; this is what an agent does when you give her your work to place. Doing this study on your own is a truly valuable learning experience, and it is to your benefit to learn the market well and find out how to keep up with it, where the information about trends and changes can be found, and where and how editorial preferences and needs originate. Later, you can reevaluate your time and needs but, right now, nothing is more important to learn than this . . . if you want to sell.

There are a few standard sources of general market news and information that are informative, reliable, and up-to-date (see Appendix V).

Guidelines.

These are printed by and available from some publishers, particularly for specific lines of books. Paperback publishers who publish original as well as reprint titles have these for their various romance series. Harper Junior Books, for another example, has a sheet called "Suggestions for Submitting Manuscripts." Cobblestones, a children's history magazine, sends to interested authors a guide sheet listing forthcoming themes. When you hear about the availability of guidelines, write for them, remembering to enclose a stamped self-addressed envelope. Collecting them can be informative, rewarding, and even sometimes amusing.

Writers' magazines.

There are two popular magazines for writers which appear monthly and can be found on most newsstands. They are *The Writer* and *Writer's Digest*. Although not specifically directed to children's book writers, they run many general articles of interest and, occasionally, some for this specialized field. There are monthly marketing reports with the most up-to-date information on changes and trends.

Writers' annuals.

The two magazine publishers noted above put out thick hardcover volumes each year that contain articles, reference material, market lists, publishers' addresses and requirements, and other related information for the active writer. *The Writer's Handbook* is published by The Writer, Inc. and *Writer's Market* is published by Writer's Digest. Just as the magazines have more similarities than differences, so do the annuals. Browse through them at the library to see which is more suited to your needs. I find the information in these books spotty, and sometimes it is difficult to distinguish adult department requirements from juvenile, but by and large these are handy references.

Trade journals.

The weekly publication of and about the publishing industry is *Publishers Weekly*. Occasionally, it contains news and articles relating to the children's book part of the industry, and devotes a page every week to reviews of new books for the bookstore buyer. Two issues a year, in February and July, are devoted to children's publishing and include previews of forthcoming spring and fall books, plus additional articles and features. The library and education fields, related by their enormous dependence on books, have their trade publications too, and while they are written from the point of view of those working in these professions, there are sometimes articles and features of great interest to the writer. Always interesting, I think, are the reviews in these publications, because they give the writer some idea of how a book is viewed by a major purchaser of children's books, with a specific set of standards and needs in mind. Some of these publications are the American Library Association's *Booklist, School Library Journal, Instructor,* and the *Bulletin of the Center for Children's Books.*

You will be amazed at how much background information you can and will pick up in these articles and reviews. Perhaps you will learn how editors decide their publishing needs and how they make difficult choices, or what makes a library buyer turn down a non-fiction book by a well-known author.

Another advantage to keeping your eyes and ears open to industry news is that you may find a second market for some of your work. Perhaps the research you did for your book on whales left you with overflowing, unused files packed with interesting information. In your readings, maybe you discover that a new children's magazine has been started, featuring the natural sciences. Try to interest the editor in an article—a feature—about whales. You may also find that other publications need fillers—anecdotes, facts, humor—and you may be able to put together some bits and pieces for them from your files.

In the previews of forthcoming books in *Publishers Weekly,* you may notice that a publisher is starting a new series of books about computers. If you have a strong interest in this area, you can query the editor about your idea before his first book on the subject is actually published.

Small publishers with specialized lines of books are emerging all the time. Maybe you will hear of one that does the kind

141

of book you want to write, about a subject you have already researched or explored, like wind surfing or city gardening or solar energy. It would be wise to keep track of these small presses; they may be looking for new writers with new projects.

Writers' organizations.

Although many of these groups insist that members be published as a requirement for joining, others are more liberal and even encourage beginning writers with information and services to help them get started. They offer newsletters to members that provide publishing news and marketing information and keep members aware of important events and legislation related to their craft. Some groups have regular meetings or annual conferences, open to members and nonmembers. Attending one or more of these can be not only inspiring but, on a practical level, can put you in closer touch with editors who may be looking for your kind of book or style. Talking to other writers, too, can lead to interesting information and possible work. You might consider joining such a group in order to keep up with news and to take advantage of the social contacts and services offered (see listing in Appendix VII).

MAKE CONTACTS

Knowing the sources of information is a large part of keeping up with your business, but it isn't the only part. You have to go out and get information or make contacts when you have a lead.

Here are several scenarios in which you could play a major part:

You find, in the "People" column of *Publishers Weekly*, that an editor who has been with one publishing house for eight years has gone to another house to start her own line of children's books, featuring game and activity books for the preschooler through the second grader. You get out your manuscript for an animal riddle book and send it to her right away.

In an interview with an editor in *School Library Journal*, you learn that the editor of a certain publishing house has a strong interest in the theater, having come from a stage background. You have a manuscript for a book of plays for young children and, hearing of this predisposition to theater, send it to this editor.

After a writers' conference you are talking with other writers and discover that there is a new magazine publisher that is featuring history for young people in an interesting monthly format. History is your special interest. You have a dozen ideas already. On the advice of another writer who has already done so, you send for the magazine's guidelines and a list of forthcoming themes for the year.

Talking with a writer friend, you learn that the various teenage romance lines publish strict guidelines for their authors. Since romances are of great interest to you, you write to the editors of each of these lines asking for a copy of their guidelines.

In a previews issue of *Publishers Weekly*, you learn that a publishing house is going to issue a series in the next year on water sports, which have suddenly become so popular that there is a need for more how-to books on them. You would love to combine your interest in water-skiing with your interest in writing, so you query the editor, saying that you have learned of this series and would love to discuss some ideas with the editor. Incidentally, you pay your own research expenses, so don't let your ideas get *too* exotic. It is true, however, that you can take these expenses as tax deductions if you are under contract for a book.

During a writing class, your teacher mentions that she thinks your picture book manuscript is ready to submit to a publisher and even recommends one to you. Before twenty-four hours have gone by, you have mailed your manuscript, freshly typed, to the editor at that house.

None of the above situations is farfetched. Some of them, in fact, are real, based on situations I have witnessed. As in all businesses there is a lot of competition, and what you do with what you've got is closely related to your success. Brushing aside valuable information is a little like saying "No, thank you" to the offer of a free ticket when you're standing on line at the box office in the rain. It takes some of the pain and frustration out of getting a foot in the door, and sometimes it's the very thing you need to get started.

SUGGESTIONS—CHAPTER 15

1. Look up the latest marketing information on children's books in at least three different sources. What would you do if you wrote science fiction? Photo essays? Teenage romances? Contemporary fiction? Easy readers? Historical adventure? How-to books?

2. Find out which magazines publish fiction for ages 8 to 12, how long the stories should be, and how much you can expect to be paid if your story is accepted.

Part Five

A PUBLISHER IN YOUR FUTURE

Good stories are not written. They are rewritten. . . .
—Phyllis A. Whitney, Writing Juvenile Stories and Novels

16

Out of the Slush Pile and into the Fire

WHAT HAPPENS AT the other end, where your manuscript is received? Is it handled with care? Is it read by anybody?

The editor's secretary or assistant generally sorts the mail each day as it comes in. Manuscripts go in one pile, known by the awful term "slush pile," and other mail in another. The secretary keeps a record, or log, of all manuscripts received each day. Sometimes an acknowledgment is sent to the author. If you want to be certain of receiving one, enclose with your material your own stamped self-addressed postcard for the secretary to check off and mail back to you.

READERS' REPORTS

The manuscript is then given to a first reader. This may be someone on the staff or a freelance outside reader with professional qualifications. All manuscripts are looked at carefully. Those that are poorly written or badly imitative will probably not get a full reading. Neither will a manuscript totally inappropriate for that publisher. No editorial staff will waste its time on something that is hopeless. However, professional readers know what to look for. If the first few pages of a novel do not work, a reader knows enough to skip ahead and read another few pages, and perhaps another few, to see if things improve. This can happen in novels, especially first novels.

The size of the manuscript is no indication of how quickly it will be read. Technically, the four-page picture book script that came in after the twenty thick novels should be read after the novels, but I remember wanting to break up the longer readings with short pieces, and therefore read some out of order. For the most part, however, your manuscript takes its place in the pecking order. Manuscripts sent in by reputable agents are treated the same as unsolicited manuscripts in some houses and read first in others. The reason for the privilege is that the agent, in some cases, has already read a manuscript and deemed it publishable, which is similar to what a first reader does. This holds a lot of weight, if the agent can be trusted, and is an aid to the editor. With agents who do not do their homework and send out manuscripts unread or not ready for publication, the practice immediately backfires and their manuscripts find their way back to the slush pile.

A written report is made up by the reader. The report includes a brief summary of the plot, an evaluation, and a recommendation. If the reader says that a manuscript is not good, it is sent back to the author, usually with a simple form letter. If the report is favorable, a second reading and maybe even a third and fourth are suggested before the manuscript ends up on the editor's desk, where the final reading and decision is made.

EDITORIAL COMMENTS

Sometimes an editor will write a personal note to the author. Perhaps he will remark that the manuscript was liked but could not be purchased for publication for some reason or another, but he would like to see more of your work. These remarks should be noted carefully. They are not made lightly, and you would be missing an important opportunity in not taking advantage of the offer. Consider the editor's point of view: he cannot buy every good manuscript he sees, but must constantly strive for variety in subject matter, style, and age group. Maybe your next story will be better suited to his needs.

Most editors are cautious about giving specific criticism unless they are ready to buy a manuscript. An author may feel that the editor's comments imply a commitment. Therefore, to avoid hurt feelings and disappointment, editors may avoid personal comments. If you should get a letter from an editor about your manuscript but without an offer of a contract, assume that the editor feels that you have a story worth some effort; it is not an offer to publish but is the help of a professional who has given his time to work with you to get your story right for publication. It would be rude to ignore this help, even if you disagree with the suggestions made. If you cannot justify the criticism, at least send a note to the editor thanking him for his time. Let him know that you disagree and will try to sell it elsewhere. Maybe a month later, his suggestions will seem less strange to you and you may want to approach him with revisions. Keep the door open if you can. If you do take his advice and make revisions, it is only fair to send the manuscript back to him for a rereading before sending it to any other publisher.

MULTIPLE REVISIONS

Occasionally, editors suggest two or more revisions, still with no offer of a contract. You will have to decide at these times whether the suggestions made are truly worth your time and consideration. Are they made for a better book or for that particular editor's personal taste? If they are personal, and there is no offer of a contract, it may not be advisable to go ahead with changes; another editor may feel differently about what is needed. If the advice helps the book considerably, and there is no question that the suggestions would improve the book, do what the editor asks. Still, if you are heading for your third revision, you should at least discuss with the editor his intent.

A publisher will rarely make a commitment to a beginning writer for anything but a finished work of fiction or a fully detailed proposal. It is possible to send a partial manuscript of a novel with the remainder summarized; a publisher may not offer you a contract, but he may let you know if he is seriously interested in the rest.

REJECTIONS

There are many manuscripts that show promise but are not bought, simply because the list isn't big enough to accommodate them, or because the work that needs to be done with the author is more than the editor's time will allow. Sometimes a perfectly good manuscript is rejected because it does not stand out in any way, has no "special" quality. It takes a good bit of self-confidence and a good critical sense to overcome the feeling of personal rejection that comes with returned manuscripts, but if you can understand decisions from the editor's point of view, you can get through rejections a lot more easily. Many writers complain that they wish that editors would say why their stories are unpublishable. The fact is publishing is a business, not a school. Editors and readers read your work for the sole purpose of finding and selecting good publishable book material so they can produce books, sell them, and make a profit for the company. They expect the work that comes to them to be of professional quality and that any help you need will have been sought *before* you submit your work. It is a fact that from 50 to 90 percent of all manuscripts received by publishers unsolicited are poorly written or submitted without regard to already existing books or the publishers' interests. Although most publishers continue to accept unsolicited manuscripts and are willing to spend time and money evaluting them, some have closed their doors to this practice, since the percentage of publishable manuscripts discovered in the "slush pile" does not warrant the expense.

CONTRACT

When a contract is offered, it is usually done by letter, or by phone, with a letter to follow. An editor may want to talk with you first, to discuss the work to be done on the manuscript. Once the editor knows how you think and what it will be like to work with you, she may offer you a contract. You will be given time to look over the contract and discuss its terms with an agent or a lawyer, if necessary.

There are different kinds of contracts. In magazine publishing and with some mass market and textbook publishers, flat-fee contracts or "work-for-hire" contracts may be offered. These carry no provision for further payments or royalties. In work-for-hire contracts, you usually agree to give up all rights to the work and the publisher copyrights in its name. Read your contract carefully to know which rights you are signing away.

Book contracts are generally standardized in form with terms, such as advance and royalty rate, to be filled in. Advances vary according to the experience of the author and how many copies of the book the publisher figures it can sell. Royalties seldom vary; 10 percent is the standard percentage allotted for author and illustrator. For a nonillustrated book, such as a teenage novel, you would receive the full 10 percent. For a picture book, where the illustrator is equally important to the book, you would probably share the royalty evenly.

As you publish more, your advances will increase, but the royalty rate remains the same. You will have to be quite a major force in children's publishing before that 10 percent is increased. A few writers have reached—and earned—more than 10 percent.

There should, ideally, be an escalation clause in your contract which states that, if your book were to sell more than a certain number of copies, your royalties would increase. If there isn't such a clause, ask about the possibility of including one. Escalation clauses are, however, extremely rare for beginning writers and even for many somewhat established ones.

Some companies have a clause stating that your royalties will be based on *net* proceeds rather than gross. This can affect your royalties considerably, so understand the contract you sign, note the terms carefully, and avoid surprises later. You can always turn down an offer if a contract seems unfair and the publisher is unwilling to negotiate.

The option clause, giving the publisher the right to your next work of a similar nature, is standard for a first book, giving the publisher the right to the work if you can agree on financial terms. Afterward, you can negotiate to remove this clause so that you are free to submit your next book to anyone you please.

EARNINGS

There is no way to guess how much money you can make on a book. A lot depends on the state of book budgets in libraries and schools, reviews, promotion and publicity, subsidiary rights sales, and plain good luck. Sales of my book, *You Can't Eat Peanuts in Church and Other Little-Known Laws,* jumped sky high when Johnny Carson read excerpts from it on the "Tonight Show."

If everything goes perfectly, you might receive an advance of $2,000 from a hardcover publisher for your first novel. If it has a catalog price of $9.95, your royalty (10 percent) will give you $.995 for each copy sold. If you sell 5,000 copies, that will be a total of $4,975. Subtract from this amount your $2,000 advance, and, in about one year, you will have earned $2,975. No taxes have been withheld.

In your second year, perhaps you sell 2,500 copies of the book; that's another $2,487.50. Perhaps you will sell the TV rights for a children's special program, giving you an additional $3,000. All of this sounds terrific, but consider that it is still below the official poverty level. The fact of the matter is, for most people, writing children's books is not a lucrative business, but there are some writers who earn their living at it. It is the kind of field in which you have to weigh the rewards of the work against the risks and struggle. Certainly, you should not consider giving up a full-time paying job at this point to stay at home and do nothing but write children's books . . . not if you have rent to pay and food to buy. If you stay with it, and find your success, you will know when the time has come to give up the other job.

SUBSIDIARY RIGHTS

These rights are all rights to your work that are offshoots of your creation. They include paperback rights, book club rights, movie and TV rights, toys and games based on characters you have created, and so forth. Publishers are automatically entitled to book rights only, including paperback and book club, within the United States and its territories. Anything else must be negotiated with you. Your agent, if you have one, will try to sell foreign rights, movie rights, and whatever else is feasible. In the absence of an agent, the publisher will act as your agent and help you to sell those rights. Let him do it: you have no way of doing this yourself.

If Five Star Movie Productions wants to buy the movie rights to your novel, *Teen Dreams*, they will come to your publisher. The publisher will direct the movie company to your agent or, if you have no agent, talk to the movie people on your behalf, consulting with you about terms. The publisher usually receives 15 percent commission for this service. If you have an agent, he receives his standard commission.

If a paperback publisher wants to buy reprint rights to your book, the hardcover publisher can negotiate the rights without your consent, because it is still *book* rights. You may be consulted about terms, but the disposition of those rights is up to the publisher. If there is an agent involved on this book, she will still receive her commission, from your part of the income on this deal.

When the time comes, read through your contract with the help of a lawyer; it isn't as "Greek" as you think. With a little effort, you can understand the various clauses so that you will know what you are talking about. A little knowledge goes a very long way.

SUGGESTIONS—CHAPTER 16

1. Be a first reader for Children's Delight Publishing Compa-
    ny, and write a reader's report on the story of either *The
    Three Little Pigs* or *Alice's Adventures in Wonderland* as
    though it were being submitted as new material today.
    Make a recommendation to the editor.

2. a. You are an editor. A manuscript comes to you for a
        novel that is poorly written and badly developed.
        Draft a letter to the author to accompany the returned
        manuscript.

    b. In the same position, you receive a very promising first
        novel, but you have all the novels you can publish for
        the next two years, and an author on your list who
        writes in a similar style. Draft a letter to the author to
        accompany the returned manuscript.

17

Your Editor: Friend or Dragon?

ONCE THE CONTRACT is out of the way and you are satisfied with your agreement, you and the editor get to work on your manuscript. Manuscripts are bought in a state considered "publishable," but often revision and polishing follow to squeeze out the best the author can do for the best book that can be.

An editor is trained to observe and will see many things that you cannot see when you are so close to your material. It can be as simple as pointing out that your heroine behaves more like a 12-year-old than an 11, or it can be more complex, like seeing that you tend to withdraw from potentially strong scenes rather than confront the emotional issues involved. Editors do not rewrite your material (if they are good editors); they make suggestions, open your eyes to new possibilities, and discuss solutions with you, but they leave the writing to you.

BE FLEXIBLE

If you disagree with an editor, and there is no satisfactory compromise, you will almost always be allowed to win your point. Be flexible and listen to what the editor is saying. You may find, after all, that there is something there. A good author will listen and bend, if necessary, even at the expense of certain favorite phrases or sections in the manuscript, if the advice is sound and the book would be improved by the change. An editor usually knows how to point things out so that the author can accept the change comfortably.

I turned in a manuscript for a picture storybook containing four little stories about two animal friends. The editor liked it, bought it, and proceeded to edit it. We had several discussions, usually about the behavior of the animals and the logistics of details. Several improvements came out of these talks. Then, quite suddenly, she made a suggestion that left me gasping.

"I think you ought to drop the first story," she said.

"How can I drop it?" I cried. "That's the story that sets up the relationship between the two friends."

"Exactly," replied my editor. "You set them up for the friendship which is perfectly clear from their actions. You don't need explanations. I think the first story slows it down. The second story starts right in, and it's obvious that they are friends. Look at it and think about it. Let me know what you think."

Needless to say, it was devastating to think about cutting out one-fourth of my book. I was attached to that story. In the next few days, going over it again and again, I saw that my editor was right. I have had cause many times since to admire her judgment. The book was published (*The Great Big Elephant and the Very Small Elephant*) in hardcover, and was subsequently published by two book clubs, in hard- and soft-cover, and by a book club in England.

(p.6)

In school, Robert Peabody called them Huey, Dewey, and Louie, and quacked whenever he saw them. "Quack, quack, quaaaaa-aaa-aaaaack!" they heard all day long.

When it was time to put on the Christmas play in school, the triplets got very excited.

"I want to play the shepherd~~ (who) sees the star~~," said Patty, who always liked being around

(p.7)

animals, even sheep.

"I want to be Herod, the wicked King," said Hattie, imagining herself in ~~the~~ a glittering ~~robe and~~ crown ~~, that she would make.~~

"I want to be the angel and fly on a wire across the stage," said Mattie, who was always the most daring.

(p.8)

Instead, Miss Vigger, their teacher, gave them the parts of the three Wise Men. They all looked alike and had nothing to do but walk across the stage.

(p.9)

Sometimes it was ~~fun~~ nice doing things together. ¶ ~~For example,~~ taking a bath was ~~good~~ lots more fun with three.

(p.10)

And the triplets could sing "Row, Row, Row Your Boat" better than anyone else.

This is a typical page in an edited manuscript. All the markings are significant within the publishing house, either for the design of the page or for the typesetter. For the author, however, the important changes are those to the text. As you can see from the editor's changes, the revisions have improved the text by eliminating unnecessary words or phrases, making it crisper and cleaner.

From *THE TRIPLETS* by Barbara Seuling, published by Houghton Mifflin/Clarion Books. Copyright © 1980 by Barbara Seuling.

WHEN YOUR EDITOR LEAVES

Occasionally, you will find an editor you like who then leaves the company for some reason or another—right in the middle of work on your book. What do you do? Some writers become so attached to their editors that they follow them wherever they go, contract permitting. If not, you must finish out your contract with the present company and perhaps sign up your next work with your old editor at her new company. You may also decide that it is worth staying at the present publishing house, even without the editor you liked, because you want the continuity of working with one house. However you deal with it, losing an editor is an unsettling experience and takes a while to get over.

Author/editor relationships can be exciting, challenging, inspirational, and productive. Most of them are, as a matter of fact, but, alas, they can also be otherwise. I have known authors to work with editors who clearly hated their work, and others who never spoke to them about it, just sent letters outlining what needed to be done, accepted revisions without a murmur, and sent the manuscript off to be produced. If you are stuck with an editor you don't like, there is very little to be done about it, but once you are finished with the present book, you are free, unless you have an option to fulfill, to look elsewhere for a publisher. Even with an option, you can turn down an offer if the terms are not satisfactory.

COPYEDITING AND GALLEYS

There comes a time, after the final revision on the manuscript, after you and your editor have achieved a satisfactory version of the book, when months have gone by without a word from your publisher. You will imagine all sorts of terrible things: your book has been postponed indefinitely; your manuscript was eaten by the editor's dog; your publishing house has gone bankrupt; they have decided to drop you and have not been able to tell you so. The truth is, the editor and the whole publishing house staff are working on dozens of other books while yours is off in the copyediting, production, or design department. Each department has the manuscript for a period of time and it is passed on to someone else, until it has gone through all the stages preparatory to publishing. You will see the copyedited manuscript with queries and corrections. You may still make changes at this point. After the type has been set, you will see galleys, or unpaged proofs, of your book for final corrections. At this time it is costly to make anything but technical corrections, so don't plan to revise in galleys. You may see an artist's sketch for your book jacket, and some flap copy or catalog copy, but other than that, nothing much happens until you see your finished book, right off the press, with your name printed boldly on the front.

The process, from signing the contract to autographing your first copy for your mother, takes at least one year, often longer.

Your chances for subsequent publication have improved considerably with this first success, and you need to feed success to keep it alive.

So, get to work! You are a professional now.

SUGGESTIONS—CHAPTER 17

Spend some time getting your tools in order. Do you have clean manila envelopes of the appropriate size? Do you have a sturdy mailing box in which to send out your novel? Is there sufficient postage on hand to send out your next manuscript, including return postage? A small investment in a postage scale may save you many trips to the post office. Do you have a few acknowledgment postcards and stamped self-addressed envelopes ready to enclose with your next manuscript? Do you have a fresh waterproof marker for addressing packages boldly and clearly?

18

Joining the Writing Community

THE ONE INGREDIENT lacking, so far, is contact with other writers on a regular basis. People with office jobs have a kind of extended family at the office, friendships are made, support is offered, information is shared.

It is important for writers to have such relationships with their colleagues, but we have to go about establishing them differently, since we write mostly in isolation.

Some writers form local groups that meet on a regular basis. They talk about their work, about their experiences with publishers, and they may even exchange manuscripts. Other groups just read works in progress for criticism. If members are spread out and must travel a good distance to attend a meeting, it can be quite a social event. One group of New England writers meets on a bimonthly basis and has grown to be good friends. Each meeting starts with a dinner, to which each person contributes a dish. Afterward, book news among the members is discussed—new contracts, published books, reviews, author tours, work problems, and so on. The rest is purely social but inevitably focuses on books, editors, and related topics. The group numbers about fifteen, and for some it is the only completely free day, away from family and other obligations, in which they can indulge in the total pleasure of being a writer among other writers.

A smaller group in New York functions more as a support group than a social or critique group. They share information and help each other over the rough spots. Still other groups invite professional people such as editors, writers, illustrators, and agents to come and talk, chipping in to pay for the visitor's honorarium. A small group with a particular interest can collaborate on a project. However you use your group, it is important because it puts you together with other writers, so that you become more informed and get away from the isolated writer's existence now and then.

To start a writers group, talk to the librarian at your local library; she may know other writers in the area. Advertise in your local paper or post notices on university or community bulletin boards. Write to publishers asking about other children's writers in your geographic area. Once you find interested people, arrange a location for the first meeting and set a date. Your first meeting will tell you in which direction you want to go, whether you will read manuscripts or talk, or whether you will deal actively with issues close to writers' hearts.

We have already talked about writers' organizations and their meetings and conferences (see Chapter 15). Through your contacts with other writers, you will have a deeper understanding of the writing business and, at the same time, feel a part of a community, which is excellent for the spirit. I have seen it happen over and over again, one writer sharing an important piece of information with another, or one writer introducing another to someone in the publishing business.

BOOK TALKS

Once you have a book published, there are other ways to meet people who have an interest in children's books, particularly yours. Go to your local public schools and libraries and speak to someone in charge about setting up book talks with children. Consider these a service to your community, during which you practice the art of the book talk until you can take your presentation further afield. Publishers often need authors who are willing to travel to various schools around the country for book fairs and author days. Once you have a good presentation worked out and understand the interchange between author and children, you can charge a fee for your talks. Since this is part of being a writer, you need not feel awkward about being paid for such jobs; you must give up writing time to do the talks and should be paid. It is only when you are learning, practicing, that you do them for nothing, or when the organization for which you do it is special to you and you do it as a favor. Publishers will help you set up book talks and take care of arranging transportation, delivery of books to sell at fairs, and other conveniences.

Promote your book in any way that you can. Fill out the questionnaire that is sent to you by your publisher's promotion department; make it interesting, lively. It is important in matching you up with requests for speaking engagements.

Keep in touch with your publisher before and after publication of your book through your editor or the publicity department. Let them know that you would like to be involved in promoting your book in any way that you can. Make it clear that you are willing to speak, grant interviews, attend autographings, appear at bookstores to help celebrate Book Week or Dr. Seuss's birthday or Halloween or whatever.

In preparation for all of this, remember to save your assorted notes, rough drafts, scraps, galleys, and any material related to the creation and production of your book. Ask the publisher to return your manuscript when he no longer needs it; an edited manuscript is always interesting to a young audience. Character sketches and anything that shows how your ideas have evolved and developed are also fascinating.

BOOK PROMOTION

Your book will be promoted in various standard ways, and perhaps some new ones. First, your book will appear in the publisher's catalog, which comes out long before the book is off the press. This catalog is sent to libraries and bookstores across the country and is given to the publisher's salespeople, who visit book buyers carrying sample books, pages, pictures, jackets, and catalogs. Twice a year the editors address the sales force directly to speak on behalf of their books. The editor tries to give the salespeople only highlights and essential information that will help in the sales representative's brief bookstore presentation.

On the road, salespeople refresh themselves on the individual books by means of an information sheet, prepared by the editors. These sheets give vital information about the book and the author. Your book is also announced in certain trade journals which are known to be read by important book buyers. Traditionally, this has been the most effective way of promoting children's books, but there is always room for change, and things could be different next year. Keep yourself informed and ask your editor questions whenever you can. If there is a house-generated publication that is sent to libraries, ask about it and how you can see that your book is mentioned in it.

Books are often bought by school and public librarians on the basis of other people's reviews, since most institutions cannot examine all the available books before purchase. Dependable sources of reviews for librarians are *School Library Journal,* the *Horn Book,* the *Bulletin of the Center for Children's Books,* and the American Library Association's *Booklist.* If a book gets poor reviews in all of these, it will not be purchased by the libraries. If two out of four don't like it, it has a limited chance. If only one doesn't like it, the damage is slight. All editors look for favorable reviews in all four, of course, for guaranteed sales.

Some library systems have book examination centers, but smaller libraries have to depend on reviews, catalogs, salespeople, or jobbers, which are companies that buy large quantities of books from all publishers and sell them to the libraries at a discount, giving the libraries one place to order from instead of dozens.

When you are talking to your editor before your book goes to press, ask if they are going to run any bookmarks or promotion pieces with your book. The art department may be able to design a simple bookmark, perhaps decorated with some illustration from your book, which can be inserted on the press sheet on which your book is printed. Bookmarks are useful when doing book talks. The children love it when you can leave them with some "souvenir" of your visit.

Haunt your local bookshop asking for your book. If it is not there, ask why it isn't, and try to get the store to order it. Do this in as pleasant a manner as possible; you want to remain on good terms with your local shop owner, be considered for autographings, and so on. If they do have your book, be sure every time you go in there to move it to a more conspicuous spot for browsers.

After six months to a year, your publisher will not be interested any longer in helping you to promote your book. This is ruled by necessity; the new books that are coming out demand the attention of the staff. You will be pretty much on your own, except for the occasional book talk that the publisher *will* help you set up. (These, with luck, can go on forever.)

SELF-PROMOTION

Instead of pouting when your "turn" is over, have a plan ready for self-promotion. Keep going around to schools and libraries; if they don't come asking for you, let them know you are available. Call a few in your area and let them know you do a dazzling presentation. Tell them your fee, the time you can spend, what you are willing to do, and how many children you can handle. Chances are you will get some positive responses. Write up a piece about your talk for the local newspaper. Use the telephone, news media, radio, and TV to help you get your book and what you do across to the public. You owe it to yourself and your book, and your publisher will be happy to work with you if you are self-sufficient in this way.

The emphasis of this book has been on book publishing, with some attention paid to magazines, since they are the traditional stepping-stones to book publishing. However, magazine publishing can be fulfilling and rewarding in its own right, especially if you are adept at short story or article writing. Textbook publishers, movie and play producers, cable TV packagers, and others also continually need fresh new children's material. Information on these related fields can be found in publications listed in Appendices V and VI.

An apprentice in any profession takes years to learn his craft. Don't be impatient if you do not begin to publish right away. The day will come when your hard work and careful study pay off. Meanwhile, enjoy learning all you can, and you will continue to grow, as a person and as a writer.

Now that you have come to the end of this book, don't stop,

whatever you do. Keep writing, and working those ideas onto paper. Follow up those leads and keep up with publishing news. Join a writers' group and talk out your frustrations as you wait for your latest manuscript to return from a publisher. Attend a writers' conference. Start something, maybe a book discussion group, at your local library. Get involved in the business of publishing and the joy of creating children's books.

I hope that you have enjoyed exploring this field with me, and that you have learned what you set out to learn. Whether you choose to pursue publication or not, I wish you luck and joy in your deeper awareness and enjoyment of children's books.

SUGGESTIONS—CHAPTER 18

1. Find out which writers' conferences will be given in the next year. Which will feature children's books? Which are in your geographic area or in a location you plan to visit? What are the requirements for attending? Write to the organization for further information.

2. Think of ways to start a writers' group that could meet locally on a regular basis. Who would you go to for help? Where would you post notices or run ads?

3. Read *How to Get Happily Published* by Judith Applebaum and Nancy Evans, about ways of promoting your book and giving it a push even without the help of the publisher.

I

Booklists

The Best of Children's Books, 1964–1978, compiled by
   Virginia Haviland and Advisory Committee at the Library
   of Congress. A listing of about 1,000 books from preschool
   to young adult, divided into categories. Superintendent of
   Documents, U.S. Government Printing Office, Washington,
   DC 20402. Specify stock number SN 030-001-00093-1.
   Inquire about prices.
Bibliography of Books for Children. Annotated listing
   updated triennially, published by the Association for
   Childhood Education International, 3615 Wisconsin
   Avenue N.W., Washington, DC 20016. Inquire about prices.
Cadecott Medal Books and *Newbery Medal Books.* Annual
   publication of the Association for Library Service to
   Children, 50 East Huron Street, Chicago, IL 60611. Single
   copy free with stamped self-addressed envelope.

Children's Books, compiled by Virginia Haviland and
Advisory Committee at the Library of Congress. Annual
listing of about 200 books from preschool through junior
high school age, classified by theme. Order from the
Superintendent of Documents, U.S. Government Printing
Office, Washington, DC 20402. Specify stock number
SN 030-001-00094-0. Inquire about price.

Children's Choices. Annotated list of books chosen by
children annually. Single copy free with stamped (2-ounce)
self-addressed envelope. "Children's Choices,"
International Reading Association, P.O. Box 8139, Newark,
DE 19711.

Choosing Books for Children: A Commonsense Guide by
Betsy Hearne. A guide to books for preschool through
young adult readers. Dell Publishing Co., 1 Dag
Hammarskjold Plaza, 245 East 47th Street, New York, NY
10017. Inquire about price.

Notable Children's Books. Annual listing available from the
Association for Library Service to Children, 50 East Huron
Street, Chicago, IL 60611, free for a stamped self-
addressed envelope.

A *Parent's Guide to Children's Reading* by Nancy Larrick.
Annotated throughout, this is for parents and anyone else
interested in books for children from preschool age to
pre-teens. Bantam Books, Inc., 414 East Golf Road,
Des Plaines, IL 60016. Inquire about price.

Picture Books for Children, edited by Patricia Jean Cianciolo
and the Picture Book Committee of the National Council
of Teachers of English. Books selected for artistic and
literary excellence. Annotated. Association of Library
Service to Children, 50 East Huron Street, Chicago, IL
60611. Inquire about price.

In addition, you local library will probably have a book list to guide you. The New York Public Library has several lists available and will send an order form on request. Many books on children's literature, such as Selma G. Lanes's *Down the Rabbit Hole,* include recommended readings for various age groups in their appendices.

171

APPENDIX

II

Children's Book Reviews

Book Review Digest, H. W. Wilson Co., 950 University Avenue, Bronx, NY 10452.

Book Review Index, Gale Research Co., Book Tower, Detroit, MI 48226.

Booklist, American Library Association, 50 East Huron Street, Chicago, IL 60611.

Bulletin of the Center for Children's Books, University of Chicago, Graduate Library School, 1100 East 57 Street, Chicago, IL 60637.

The Horn Book, 31 St. James Avenue, Boston, MA 02116.

New York Times Book Review, 229 West 43 Street, New York, NY 10036.

Publishers Weekly, R. R. Bowker Company, 205 E. 42nd Street, New York, NY 10017.

School Library Journal, R. R. Bowker Company, 205 E. 42nd Street, New York, NY 10017.

III

About Children's Literature—History and Criticism

Books, Children, and Men, Paul Hazard. Translated by Marguerite Mitchell. The Horn Book, 1944. Reissued, 1960.

Children and Books, May Hill Arbuthnot. Scott, Foresman and Company, 1964.

A Critical History of Children's Literature, Cornelia Meigs, ed., Macmillan, 1953.

Down the Rabbit Hole, Selma G. Lanes. Atheneum, 1971.

From Childhood to Childhood, Jean Karl. John Day, 1970.

The History of Children's Literature, Elva S. Smith. American Library Association, 1937.

Little Wide-Awake: An Anthology of Victorian Children's Books and Periodicals, selected by Leonard de Vries. World Publishing Company, 1967.

A St. Nicholas Anthology, selected and edited by Burton C. Frye. Meredith Press, 1969.

A Sense of Story, John Rowe Townsend. Lippincott, 1971.

Summoned by Books, Frances Clarke Sayres. Viking Press, 1965.

Three Centuries of Children's Books in Europe, Bettina Hürlimann. World Publishing Company, 1968.

The Unreluctant Years, Lillian Smith. American Library Association, 1953. Viking Compass edition (paper), 1967.

IV

Reference Books—
Directories, Manuals,
and Guides

Books from Writer to Reader, Howard Greenfeld, Crown,
1976. A clear account of how books are created and
produced.
Elements of Style, William Strunk, Jr., and E. B. White,
Macmillan. 3rd ed., 1979. A classic and a must for all
writers. In paperback.
Finding Facts Fast, Alden Todd, Ten Speed Press. 2nd ed.,
1979. Useful directions on how to find out what you want
to know.
How to Get Happily Published, Judith Applebaum and
Nancy Evans, Harper & Row, 1978. About promoting your
book with and without the help of your publisher.
Literary Market Place ("LMP"), R. R. Bowker Company.
Annual director of publishing information. Names and
addresses of publishers, agents, book reviewers, book clubs,
associations, typing services, and anything else to do with
the industry.

Members List, Children's Book Council, Inc., 67 Irving Place, New York, NY 10003. A handy list, yours for the asking plus a stamped self-addressed envelope. Includes addresses, phone numbers, editors' names.

Pocket Pal: A Graphic Arts Production Handbook, International Paper Company. An introduction to printing processes, color reproduction, graphic arts, and book production.

Publishers' Trade List Annual, R. R. Bowker Company. A collection of catalogs of the major publishers, arranged alphabetically.

The Reader's Guide to Periodical Literature, H. W. Wilson. An index by author, subject, and title to the leading magazines.

Reference Books: A Brief Guide, Enoch Pratt Free Library. A guide to source materials. Updated periodically.

Subject Guide to Books in Print, Subject Guide to Children's Books in Print, and *Books in Print,* R. R. Bowker Company. Thorough indexes by subject, title, and author to all books currently in print.

The Word Processing Book, Peter A. McWilliams. A short course in computer literacy, as applied to the writer interested in moving from the typewriter to the word processor.

A Writer's Guide to Copyright, Poets & Writers, Inc., 1979. A summary of the copyright law today, writers' rights and how to execute them, copyright registration.

The Writer's Handbook, The Writer, Inc. "How-to" articles and market information.

Writer's Market, Writer's Digest, Inc. Information on markets, agents, and other concerns of the freelance writer.

V

Where You Can Find Marketing Information

Organization Newsletters. Most writers' organizations publish regular bulletins or newsletters for members which include marketing information focusing on the specialty of the organization. The Society of Children's Book Writers, for example, prepares and updates regularly a marketing survey for its members that is available with membership free of charge. The Authors Guild Bulletin contains marketing and publishing news. *Coda,* the publication of Poets & Writers, Inc., offers many articles on marketing poetry and fiction. Although you must be a member to take advantage of these offerings, you may find that the cost of membership dues is worth the valuable information that you will receive on a regular basis.

The Trade Journals. Publications such as *Publishers Weekly* and the *Horn Book* will occasionally provide insights into a marketing phenomenon or new trends, although they do

not directly deal with marketing information for the
writer. (See Appendix II for details of these journals.)

The Writer, 8 Arlington Street, Boston, MA 02116. Monthly,
with a regular "Market Newsletter" and special market
lists throughout the year. Writing for children's and young
adult magazines is featured in April; book publishers are
covered in July.

Writer's Digest, 9933 Alliance Road, Cincinnati, OH 45242.
Monthly, with market reports from various regions.
Informational articles and pieces on the concerns of
writers. Occasional articles especially for children's writers.

The Writer's Handbook, an annual compendium of articles,
marketing information, and directories to publishers of all
kinds. Published by The Writer, Inc., 8 Arlington Street,
Boston, MA 02116.

Writer's Market, published by Writer's Digest, 9933 Alliance
Road, Cincinnati, OH 45242, is similarly composed of
informational material for the working writer, complete
with marketing lists.

The Writers' Magazines. In addition to the information
packed into the monthly issues, the publishers of the
magazines offer a good number of books on specific
markets. A listing of these will be sent to you on request.

VI

Books on the
Writing Craft

IN GENERAL—THE CRAFT OF WRITING

Becoming a Writer, Dorothea Brand. J. B. Tarcher,
1981.

Fiction Writer's Handbook, Hallie & Whit Burnett. Barnes &
Noble, 1975.

How to Write Plots That Sell, F. A. Rockwell. Contemporary
Books, Inc., 1975.

On Writing Well, William Zinsser. Harper & Row,
1976.

Secrets of Successful Fiction, Robert Newton Peck. Writer's
Digest Books, 1980.

Techniques of the Selling Writer, Dwight V. Swain.
University of Oklahoma Press, 1974.

Writing a Novel, John Braine. McGraw-Hill, 1975.

Writing and Selling Non-fiction, Hayes Jacobs. Writer's
Digest, 1975.

ON WRITING FOR CHILDREN

The Children's Picture Book: How to Write It, How to Sell It,
Ellen E. M. Roberts. Writer's Digest, 1981.

*Dinosaurs and Rainbows: Creating and Selling Non-fiction
for Children,* Ellen E. M. Roberts. Writer's Digest, 1984.

How to Write for Children and Young Adults, Jane Fitz-
Randolph. Barnes & Noble Books, 1980. (Originally
Writing for the Juvenile and Teenage Market, Funk &
Wagnalls.)

Writing Books for Children, Jane Yolen. The Writer, Inc.,
1976.

Writing for Children and Teenagers, Lee Wyndham. Revised
by Arnold Madison. Writer's Digest Books, 1980.

Writing for Young Children, Claudia Lewis. Doubleday,
1954. Revised, 1981.

Writing Juvenile Stories and Novels, Phyllis A. Whitney. The
Writer, Inc., 1976.

Writing Mysteries for Young People, Joan Lowery Nixon. The
Writer, Inc., 1977.

*Writing With Pictures: How to Write and Illustrate Children's
Books,* Uri Shulevitz. Watson-Guptill Publications, 1985.

Note: the book that is just right for you depends on what you
want from it. Look at as many of the above books as you can
find (they are all in print as of this writing). No doubt you will
find Phyllis Whitney's book more useful than Claudia Lewis's if
you are interested in older novels; if your main interest is
picture books, the Lewis book is a classic on the genre, and you
will want to see Ellen Roberts's book as well. Each of the titles
above will have specific features and reflect the major
strengths of its author.

BY AND ABOUT THE CREATORS OF CHILDREN'S BOOKS

Authors and Illustrators of Children's Books, Miriam
Hoffman and Eva Samuels. R. R. Bowker Company, 1972.

Books Are by People, Lee Bennett Hopkins. Citation Press, 1969.

Gates of Excellence, Katherine Paterson. E. P. Dutton, 1981.

The Green and Burning Tree, Eleanor Cameron. Atlantic-Little Brown, 1969.

Questions to an Artist Who Is Also an Author: A Conversation Between Maurice Sendak and Virginia Haviland. Library of Congress, 1972. Reprinted from the Library's Quarterly Journal, vol. 28, no. 4 (October 1971).

VII

Organizations for the Writer of Children's Books

The Society of Children's Book Writers, Box 296, Los Angeles, CA 90066. A national organization of children's writers and illustrators, founded in 1968, devoted to the interests of children's literature. Sponsors the Golden Kite Award for excellence in children's books, annually. Holds writers' conferences in several regions and publishes a bimonthly bulletin for members. Assorted literature on such topics as contracts and agents is offered free to members.

The Children's Book Council, Inc., 67 Irving Place, New York, NY 10003. A nonprofit trade association of children's book publishers, promoting the reading and enjoyment of children's books. Issues a calendar of book-related events and various promotion pieces. Publications about submitting manuscripts, publishers' lists, and illustrators' aides are available on request for a stamped self-addressed

envelope. The library is open to the public for browsing
and research.

The Authors League of America, Inc., 234 West 44 Street,
New York, NY 10036. Promotes the professional interests
of authors and is actively involved in initiating and
supporting legislation to protect authors from unfair taxes,
unsatisfactory copyright protection, and infringement of
the right to free expression.

PEN American Center, 47 Fifth Avenue, New York, NY
10003. An international organization of writers dedicated
to bringing about better understanding among writers of
all nations. Actively involved in the rights and freedom of
all writers.

Poets & Writers, Inc., 201 West 54 Street, New York, NY
10019. An organization of poets and fiction writers.
Publishes useful guides for the writer on topics of concern:
literary agents, sponsors, copyright, and so on.

There are many other organizations and associations for
writers and others in the arts. These are just a few. Look in
Literary Market Place for a more complete listing. Send for
information about membership and dues; some groups require
that you be published in order to join, others that you are a
specific kind of writer (mysteries, poetry, and so on). It is
important to compare the different organizations to discover
which one suits your needs.

VIII

Readings
for the Illustrator

All Mirrors Are Magic Mirrors: Reflections on Pictures Found in Children's Books, Welleran Poltarnees. Green Tiger Press, 1972.

American Picture Books from Noah's Ark to the Beast Within, Barbara Bader. Macmillan, 1976.

The Art of Art for Children's Books, Diana Klemin. Clarkson N. Potter, Inc., 1966.

The Art of Maurice Sendak, Selma G. Lanes. Harry N. Abrams, 1980.

The Art of the Picture Book, Walter Lorraine, ed. Wilson Library Bulletin, October 1977.

Authors and Illustrators of Children's Books, Miriam Hoffman and Eva Samuels. R. R. Bowker Company, 1972.

Bookmaking: The Illustrated Guide to Design/Production/Editing, 2nd ed., Marshall Lee. R. R. Bowker Company, 1979.

Books Are by People, Lee Bennett Hopkins. Citation Press, 1969.

Books from Writer to Reader, Howard Greenfeld. Crown, 1976.

The Child's First Books: A Critical Study of Pictures and Texts, Donnarae MacCann and Olga Richard. H. W. Wilson, 1973.

Children and Books, May Hill Arbuthnot. Scott, Foresman and Company, 1964.

Children's Books and Their Illustration, Gerald Gottlieb. David Godine, 1975.

The Children's Picture Book, Ellen E. M. Roberts. Writer's Digest, 1981.

Down the Rabbit Hole, Selma G. Lanes. Atheneum, 1971.

From Childhood to Childhood: Children's Books and Their Creators, Jean Karl. John Day, 1970.

The Graphics Artists Handbook: Pricing and Ethical Guidelines, The Graphic Artists Guild.

Illustrating Children's Books, Henry C. Pitz. Watson-Guptill, 1963.

Illustrating the Little House Books, Garth Williams. The Horn Book Magazine, December 1953.

Illustrations in Children's Books, Patricia Cianciolo. William C. Brown Co., 1970.

The Illustrator's Notebook, Lee Kingman, ed. The Horn Book, Inc., 1978.

Illustrators of Books for Young People, Martha E. Ward and Dorothy A. Marquardt. 2nd ed. Scarecrow, 1975.

Illustrators of Children's Books, 1744–1945, Bertha E. Mahoney, Louise Payson Latimer, and Beulah Folmsbee, compilers. The Horn Book, Inc., 1947.

Illustrators of Children's Books, 1946–1956, Ruth Hill Viguers, Marcia Dalphin, and Bertha Mahoney Miller, compilers. The Horn Book, Inc., 1958.

Illustrators of Children's Books, 1957–1966, Lee Kingman, Joanna Foster, and Ruth Giles Lontoft, compilers. The Horn Book, Inc., 1968.

Illustrators of Children's Books, 1967–1976, Lee Kingman, Grace Allen Hogarth, and Harriet Quimby, compilers. The Horn Book, Inc., 1978.

Picture-Book World, Bettina Hürlimann, translated and edited by Brian W. Alderson. Oxford University Press, 1968.

Publishing Children's Books in America, 1919–1976: An Annotated Bibliography, Robin Gottlieb. The Children's Book Council, 1978.

Questions to an Artist Who Is Also an Author: A Conversation Between Maurice Sendak and Virginia Haviland. Library of Congress, 1972. Reprinted from the Library's Quarterly Journal, vol. 28, no. 4 (October 1971).

Robert Lawson, Illustrator: A Selection of His Characteristic Illustrations, with Introduction and Comment by Helen L. Jones. Little, Brown and Company, 1972.

Writing, Illustrating and Editing Children's Books, Jean Poindexter Colby. Hastings House, 1967.

Writing With Pictures: How to Write and Illustrate Children's Books, Uri Shulevitz. Watson-Guptill Publications, 1985.

Index

187